Home Baking

CAKES • COOKIES • PIES • PASTRIES • BREAD

Home Baking

CAKES · COOKIES · PIES · PASTRIES · BREAD

p

This is a Parragon Publishing book

This edition published in 2005

Parragon Publishing
Queen Street House
4 Queen Street
Bath BA1 1HE, UK

Copyright © Parragon 2003

ISBN: 1-40544-760-5

Printed in China

This edition designed by Shelley Doyle

Photography and text by The Bridgewater Book Company Ltd

Cover Photography by Mark Wood

Cover Home Economist Pamela Gwyther

NOTES FOR THE READER

This book uses imperial, metric or US cup measurements. Follow the same units of measurement throughout;
do not mix imperial and metric.

All spoon measurements are level: teaspoons are assumed to be 5 ml, and tablespoons are assumed to be 15 ml.

Unless otherwise stated, milk is assumed to be whole and eggs are medium.

Recipes using raw or very lightly cooked eggs should be avoided by infants, the elderly, pregnant women,
convalescents and anyone suffering from an illness.

Optional ingredients, variations or serving suggestions have not been included in the calculations. The times given are
an approximate guide only. Preparation times differ according to the techniques used by different people and the
cooking times may also vary from those given.

Contents

Introduction 6

Family Treats 10

Sweet Delights 56

Savory Bites 94

Festive Feasts 122

Special Day Bakes 172

Index 175

Introduction

Baking is just about the most satisfying type of cooking there is. Perhaps it's the aroma of fresh croissants as they emerge from the oven, the rewarding pleasure of cutting into a homemade Christmas cake, or the comforting knowledge that a plate of irresistible brownies awaits the kids when they return from school. Whatever the reason, home baking is probably the world's best therapy as it always makes you feel good about yourself–and family and friends will share that opinion too.

From pies and tarts to muffins and cookies and from simple sponge cakes to elaborate gateaux, this book is packed with recipes to suit all tastes and every occasion, whatever your level of skill, family budget, and available time. You don't have to spend hours in the kitchen to whisk up a batch of tasty cookies or savory cheese biscuits that will easily surpass the store-bought varieties. Traditional Apple Pie (see page 28) is a quick, easy, and inexpensive dessert that is the perfect end to Sunday lunch with the family, while those who have more time to lavish on preparing an elegant dinner party treat might like to delight their guests with a rich Dark & White Chocolate Torte (see page 136). There are also lots of recipes that look impressive but are astonishingly simple to make.

The recipes are divided into four main section– Family Treats, Sweet Delights, Savory Bites, and Festive Feasts–making it simple to find exactly the right cake or bake that you need. However, you don't have to follow this demarcation slavishly. For example, while Lemon Meringue Pie (see page 32) is a great family favorite, it would also be a good choice for an informal supper party and there's no reason why you have to wait until Christmas to enjoy the deliciously moist gingerbread Lebkuchen (see page 162). Sun-dried Tomato Rolls (see page 100) would be as welcome in a picnic basket as they are on the dinner table, while Shortbread Fantails (see page 84) are equally good with morning coffee and with ice cream at the end of lunch. The final section of the book is the place to go for just such mix-and-match ideas. Four sub-sections–Morning Coffee with Friends, Afternoon Tea with the Family, Kids' Party Time, and An Occasion to Impress–offer lots of helpful suggestions for these familiar occasions

Essential equipment

Measuring: Accurate measurement of the ingredients is essential for success with home baking. Dry ingredients, such as flour and sugar, should be weighed precisely on kitchen scales or measured accurately in standard American cups. Liquids, such as water and milk, should be measured in a graduated jug or standard measuring cups. Small quantities of both liquid and dry ingredients, such as vanilla extract and grated lemon rind, should be measured in standard spoons.

Kitchen scales may be electronic, spring, or balance. The first are quite expensive but extremely accurate. It is worth keeping spare batteries in stock. Spring scales are less expensive and very practical, although if the spring breaks it cannot be repaired. Old-fashioned balance scales look lovely in a traditional kitchen but are not so easy to use or so convenient as other types.

Measuring cups are usually sold in sets of 1, $1/2$, $1/3$, and $1/4$ cup. Those designed specifically for measuring liquids have the amount printed just below the rim of the cup to avoid spillage. Cups for measuring dry ingredients must be filled completely and can also be used for liquids providing you have a steady hand. To measure dry ingredients, overfill the cup, then level the surface with the blade of a knife.

Measuring jugs may be made of plastic or glass and are usually heatproof, but do check. If they are clear, it is easier to see the level. Always measure at eye level. The jugs are usually graduated in both metric and imperial measurements.

A set, or better still, several sets of measuring spoons are invaluable as ordinary tableware is not standard in size. Sets usually consist of $1/4$, $1/2$ and 1 teaspoon, plus 1 tablespoon. Some also include $1/8$ teaspoon and $1/2$ tablespoon. Spoons with long handles are particularly useful for reaching inside spice jars. As with measuring dry ingredients in cups, spoons should be overfilled and then levelled with the blade of a knife.

Sifting: Even ready-sifted flours should be sifted again before use in fine baking. A medium or large bowl-shaped strainer with a fine mesh is suitable for sifting into a bowl and one with a lip that will rest on the rim is best. A smaller strainer – about 4 in in diameter–is useful for sifting small quantities of confectioners' sugar and unsweetened cocoa powder for decoration. You can use metal or nylon for most baking purposes but if you are sifting fruit to remove the seeds, for example, nylon is better as it doesn't react with the acid in the fruit.

A flour dredger is not essential but it does help to spread flour evenly on a counter before pastry is rolled out. A sugar dredger is useful for sprinkling the tops of pies before or after baking. Make sure that the sugar crystals are brushed off the top of the container after refilling as you will find it impossible to unscrew the top again if they have stuck to the thread.

Mixing: Most kitchens contain a range of bowls and you can use glass, stainless steel, plastic, aluminum, or earthenware for almost all baking purposes. However, neither plastic nor aluminum is suitable for whisking egg whites. Copper is the perfect choice for really successful meringue. A ceramic bowl is ideal for pastry as it helps to keep the mixture cold. Make sure you use a bowl of the appropriate size that allows plenty of room for stirring and/or beating.

Wooden spoons with curved and straight sides are invaluable, especially for stirring liquids while they are heating. The handles may be used for shaping cookies while they are still warm from the oven.

A balloon whisk can be used for most whisking purposes and is very efficient. A flat whisk is helpful when whisking small quantities, such as an egg yolk glaze. A long, thin whisk will enable you to beat a mixture in a pitcher but is not essential.

An electric mixer, especially if it is supplied with dough hooks as well as whisks, saves time and effort.

A flexible spatula is the perfect tool for scraping cake batters out of the bowl and into a pan and for folding in beaten mixtures without destroying their aeration.

Pastry-making tools: Rolling pins may be made of metal, wood, or marble. Both metal and marble help to keep the dough cold, but marble is extremely heavy. Plastic and glass rolling pins that can be filled with cold water are also available. Some designs have handles, some don't. It doesn't really matter which you choose, but if you tend to be heavy-handed, then a rolling pin with handles is probably a better choice.

You can roll out pastry on any smooth surface and a pastry board is not essential. However, a marble board does help to keep the dough cold and needs only light flouring.

A metal pastry blender is used to rub the fat into flour. It helps to keep the mixture cool, but many cooks prefer to use their fingertips.

A pastry brush is a useful, multi-purpose tool. It can be used for brushing glaze over a pie, brushing the edges of pastry before sticking them together, and for brushing a pan with oil or melted butter to prevent the mixture from sticking.

A wide variety of cutters is available. Plain and fluted round cutters are perfect for tartlets and cookies. It's worth buying a set of at least three different sizes. Cutters with handles produce a more even pressure. They may be made of plastic or metal. Plastic doesn't rust, but metal cutters are sharper and won't rust if thoroughly dried after washing. Novelty shapes, such as Christmas trees, hearts, gingerbread figures, and moons, are also available. These are mainly used for biscuits cookies.

A pastry wheel is useful for making a decorative edge when cutting out dough, particularly for lattice strips. You can also buy a lattice cutter, but this is far from essential.

Tins, dishes and trays: All the cake recipes in this book specify both size and shape of the pan. If you use a different size pan or a rectangular pan rather than a round one, the cake may not rise properly or maybe disappointing in some other way. It is worth buying good-quality, heavy-gauge pans that will prevent scorching and will not distort. This is especially important for rich fruit cakes. They are available with a loose base to make it easier to remove the cake after baking. Non-stick linings are great for layer cake pans, although they will still require greasing before use. They are also good for deeper light sponge cakes. A springform pan, with a clip that can be loosened for unmolding the cake, saves a lot of worry if you are baking a fragile confection for a special occasion. Cake pans are available in a variety of shapes from ring molds to hearts.

Bun trays, popover trays, and muffin pans are useful for making small cakes and tartlets. Again it is worth buying good-quality cookware–non-stick if you like–which will last a lifetime. The size and number of the individual cups vary, so check the recipe before you start.

Loaf pans are rectangular and variable in size. They are available in a variety of materials and may be non-stick. Heavy-gauge, oxidized steel is very reliable.

Quiche pans may be loose-based or solid. The former are used for tarts baked with a filling so that they can be lifted out easily. The latter are used for cooking the base, which is then turned out and left to cool. It can then be filled–still upside down–with fruit, whipped cream, etc. Both kinds of pans are available in different sizes and depths.

Pie dishes are traditionally ceramic and often very attractive. This material allows the heat to penetrate to the center of the pie without the crust becoming overcooked. Make sure that the dish has a flat rim.

A heavy cookie sheet is invaluable for meringues and cookies as the heat is distributed quickly and evenly to produce a crisp result. Some have a lip on one long side, while others have a rim all the way around.

Other equipment: A metal spatula is useful for smoothing the surface of cake batter and for applying and smoothing frosting. Strong nylon pastry bags with a selection of tips are necessary if you enjoy decorating cakes, although you can also make a disposable bag from a cone of waxed paper. A variety of other kitchen gadgets, such as a cookie press, bird-shaped pie support, or shortbread mold, while not essential can be fun to have–put them on your birthday or wedding gift list.

Pointers to perfection

Although, as with all cooking, some recipes are a little more demanding than others, baking–whether cakes, pies, savory nibbles, bread, or cookies–is not particularly difficult. Certainly, the "average" cook will find all the recipes in this book within his or her scope and even beginners will be able to master many of them more or less immediately. However, there are a few extra tips worth bearing in mind to avoid disappointment.

- Always read the recipe through and collect the measured ingredients together before you start cooking.

- Take care if you substitute ingredients as the substitute may seem similar but have different properties. In most cases, soft margarine, for example, cannot be successfully substituted for block margarine or butter.

- Preheat the oven to the specified temperature. This usually takes about 15 minutes and the recipe will indicate the appropriate stage in the method.

- Check the "use-by" dates on pantry ingredients, such as flour and nuts, which can turn rancid over time.

- Don't cut corners to try to save time, as this will often end in failure. For example, a mixture may need to be chilled in the refrigerator to make it easier to roll out and handle and to guarantee a crisp texture when cooked. Similarly, if a pre-cooked filling needs to be completely cold before being topped with dough, leave plenty of time to avoid a soggy disappointment.

- Mix cake batters until they are just mixed–you will soon be able to recognize this point. If, for example, the flour is not completely folded into a whisked mixture, the dry pockets formed will cause the cake to crack during baking. Unfortunately, overmixing is likely to have the same result.

- Grease or grease and line a pan if the recipe specifies. However, if you use baking parchment, rather than waxed paper, greasing may not be necessary. Baking parchment is an especially good choice if you are baking meringue.

- Place whatever you are baking in the center of a conventional oven, unless the recipe specifies otherwise. Avoid opening the door during cooking, especially if you are baking a delicate cake, which may be prone to collapse if exposed to a cold draft.

- Follow the instructions for cooling cakes and cookies. Some should be turned out on to a wire cooling rack straightaway, while others need to remain in the pan or on the cookie sheet for a few minutes first to allow them to firm up slightly. Very rich cakes are often left to cool completely in the pan before unmolding.

- Store cakes and cookies in separate airtight containers. They will usually keep for a few days, although rich fruit cake can be stored for much longer. In the unlikely event of any cake being left over after it has been cut, wrap it in foil before returning to an airtight container. Cakes destined for decoration with fruit or cream should be stored undecorated or they will become soggy. They can be kept briefly in the refrigerator and served chilled or brought back to room temperature to serve.

- Finally, if things do go wrong, be imaginative. You will be surprised by what can be disguised with whipped cream and fresh or canned fruit. Cut off any sad pieces–sunken or burnt–and cover the remainder. Make the most of ready-to-roll frosting, shredded coconut, confectioners' sugar, chocolate sprinkles, or whatever else seems a good idea. Cakes that have broken on unmolding can be used as the basis for a delicious homemade trifle or stamped into shapes with cookie cutters.

Family Treats

This chapter is packed with traditional favorites from classic

British Bakewell Tart (see page 33) to the mouthwatering American Double

Chocolate Brownies (see page 52). There's something for everyone from

grandmas to toddlers, including plenty of lovely sticky desserts and cakes

that will appeal to kids of all ages. The emphasis throughout is on fabulous

flavor combined with ease of preparation. Even the children in the family

will probably enjoy helping to make Fruity Flapjacks (see page 50) or

Gingerbread People (see page 46). This is everyday baking at its best –

it looks great, tastes wonderful, and won't break the bank. But beware –

you may well find that your home has become a scrumptious social center

for coffee mornings, after-school homework clubs, unexpected midweek

guests, regular weekend visits from the extended family, and old-fashioned

tea parties. Of course, you'll never have any problems with leftovers.

Victoria Sponge

SERVES: 8

PREP: 10 MINS +
20 MINS
COOLING

COOKING: 25-30 MINS

Ingredients

6 oz/175 g butter, softened,
plus extra for greasing

1¼ cups self-rising flour

1 tsp baking powder

scant 1 cup golden superfine sugar

3 eggs

FILLING

3 tbsp raspberry jelly

2½ cups heavy cream, whipped

16 fresh strawberries, halved

superfine sugar, for dusting

Preheat the oven to 350°F/180°C, then grease and line the bottoms of 2 x 8-inch/20-cm sponge cake pans. Sift the flour and baking powder into a bowl and add the butter, sugar, and eggs. Mix together, then beat well until smooth.

Divide the batter evenly between the prepared pans and smooth the surfaces. Bake in the preheated oven for 25-30 minutes, or until well risen and golden brown, and the cakes feel springy when lightly pressed.

Let cool in the pans for 5 minutes, then turn out and peel off the lining paper. Transfer to wire racks to cool completely. Join the cakes together with the raspberry jelly, whipped heavy cream, and strawberry halves. Sprinkle the superfine sugar on top and serve.

Carrot Cake

SERVES: 8

PREP: 15 MINS + 20 MINS COOLING/ STANDING

COOKING: 1 HR 5 MINS

Ingredients

butter, for greasing

scant 1 cup brown sugar

3 eggs

¾ cup sunflower or corn oil

1 cup coarsely grated carrots

2 ripe bananas, mashed

⅓ cup chopped walnuts

2 cups all-purpose flour

½ tsp salt

1 tsp baking soda

2 tsp baking powder

FROSTING

scant 1 cup cream cheese

½ tsp vanilla extract

generous 1 cup confectioners' sugar

2 tbsp chopped walnuts

Preheat the oven to 350°F/180°C. Grease and line the bottom of a 9-inch/23-cm springform cake pan. Place the sugar, eggs, sunflower oil, carrots, bananas, and walnuts in a bowl. Sift in the flour, salt, baking soda, and baking powder. Beat the batter until smooth.

Turn the batter into the prepared pan and bake in the preheated oven for 1 hour 5 minutes, or until well risen and golden brown and a skewer inserted into the center comes out clean. Let cool in the pan for 10 minutes, then turn out and peel off the lining paper. Transfer to a wire rack to cool completely.

To make the frosting, place the cream cheese and vanilla extract in a bowl and beat well to soften. Beat in the confectioners' sugar a tablespoon at a time, until smooth. Swirl over the cake and sprinkle the chopped walnuts on top. Let stand in a cool place for the frosting to harden slightly before serving.

Coffee Streusel Cake

SERVES: 8

PREP: 50 MINS

COOKING: 1 HR

Ingredients

½ *cup butter, melted and cooled,*
  plus extra for greasing

2 *cups all-purpose flour*

1 *tbsp baking powder*

⅓ *cup superfine sugar*

⅔ *cup milk*

2 *eggs*

2 *tbsp instant coffee mixed with*
1 *tbsp boiling water*

⅓ *cup chopped almonds*

confectioners' sugar, for dusting

TOPPING

½ *cup self-rising flour*

⅓ *cup raw brown sugar*

2 *tbsp butter, diced*

1 *tsp ground allspice*

1 *tbsp water*

Grease a 9-inch/23-cm loose-based round cake pan with butter and line with baking parchment. Strain the flour and baking powder into a mixing bowl, then stir in the superfine sugar.

Whisk the milk, eggs, melted butter, and coffee mixture together and pour onto the dry ingredients. Add the chopped almonds and mix lightly together. Spoon the mixture into the prepared pan.

To make the topping, combine the flour and raw brown sugar in a bowl.

Rub in the butter with your fingertips until the mixture resembles bread crumbs. Sprinkle in the allspice and water and bring the mixture together into loose crumbs. Sprinkle evenly over the cake batter.

Bake the cake in a preheated oven, 375°F/190°C, for about 50 minutes-1 hour. Cover loosely with foil if the topping starts to brown too quickly. Let the cake cool in the pan, then turn out, dust with confectioners' sugar, and serve.

Mississippi Mud Cake

SERVES: 16

PREP: 25 MINS +
30 MINS
COOLING

COOKING: 1 HR 30 MINS

Ingredients

*8 oz/225 g butter, cut into pieces,
    plus extra for greasing*

5½ oz/150 g semisweet chocolate

*generous 2 cups golden
    superfine sugar*

1 cup hot water

3 tbsp Tia Maria or cognac

1¾ cups all-purpose flour

1 tsp baking powder

¼ cup unsweetened cocoa

2 eggs, beaten

TO DECORATE

fresh raspberries

chocolate curls

Preheat the oven to 325°F/160°C, then grease and line an 8-inch/20-cm round cake pan. Break the chocolate into pieces, then place the butter, chocolate, sugar, hot water, and Tia Maria in a large, heavy-bottom pan over low heat and stir until the chocolate melts.

Stir until smooth, transfer the mixture to a large bowl, and let cool for 15 minutes. Sift in the flour, baking powder, and cocoa and whisk in, then whisk in the eggs. Pour the batter into the prepared cake pan.

Bake in the preheated oven for 1½ hours, or until risen and firm to the touch. Let cool in the pan for 30 minutes, then turn out and peel off the lining paper. Transfer to a wire rack to cool completely. Decorate with fresh raspberries and chocolate curls and serve.

Preserved Ginger Cake

SERVES: 12

PREP: 20 MINS +
1 HR
COOLING

COOKING: 45-50 MINS

Ingredients

4 oz/115 g butter, plus extra
 for greasing

generous 1½ cups self-rising flour

1 tbsp ground ginger

1 tsp ground cinnamon

½ tsp baking soda

generous ½ cup brown sugar

grated rind of ½ lemon

2 eggs

1½ tbsp corn syrup

1½ tbsp milk

TOPPING

6 pieces of preserved ginger, plus
 4 tbsp ginger syrup from the jar

generous 1 cup confectioners' sugar

lemon juice

Preheat the oven to 325°F/160°C. Grease and line the bottom of a 7-inch/18-cm square cake pan. Sift the flour, ginger, cinnamon, and baking soda into a bowl. Rub in the butter, then stir in the sugar and lemon rind. Make a well in the center. Place the eggs, syrup, and milk in a separate bowl and whisk together. Pour into the dry ingredients and beat until smooth.

Pour the batter into the prepared pan and bake in the preheated oven for 45-50 minutes, or until well risen and firm to the touch. Let cool in the pan for 30 minutes, then turn out onto a wire rack and peel off the lining paper. Let cool completely.

To make the topping, cut each piece of preserved ginger into quarters and arrange the pieces on top of the cake. Sift the confectioners' sugar into a bowl and stir in the ginger syrup and enough lemon juice to make a smooth frosting. Place the frosting in a plastic bag and cut a tiny hole in one corner. Drizzle the frosting over the cake. Let set, then cut the cake into squares and serve.

Rich Fruit Cake

Ingredients

butter, for greasing

1 cup pitted unsweetened dates

¾ cup no-soak dried prunes

*scant 1 cup unsweetened
  orange juice*

2 tbsp molasses

1 tsp finely grated lemon rind

1 tsp finely grated orange rind

*1½ cups whole-wheat self-rising
  flour*

1 tsp ground allspice

¾ cup seedless raisins

¾ cup golden raisins

¾ cup currants

¾ cup dried cranberries

3 large eggs, separated

TO DECORATE

1 tbsp apricot jelly, warmed

confectioners' sugar, for dusting

6 oz/175 g sugarpaste

strips of orange rind

strips of lemon rind

Grease and line a deep 8 inch/20-cm round cake pan. Chop the dates and prunes and place in a large, heavy-bottom pan. Pour over the orange juice and let simmer for 10 minutes. Remove the pan from the heat and beat the fruit mixture until puréed. Add the molasses and citrus rinds and let cool.

Preheat the oven to 325°F/160°C. Sift the flour and spice into a bowl, adding any bran that remains in the strainer. Add the dry fruits. When the date and prune mixture is cool, whisk in the egg yolks. Whisk the egg whites in a clean bowl until stiff. Spoon the fruit mixture into the dry ingredients and mix together.

Gently fold in the egg whites. Transfer to the prepared pan and bake in the preheated oven for 1½ hours. Let cool in the pan.

Remove the cake from the pan and brush the top with jelly. Dust the counter with confectioners' sugar and roll out the sugarpaste thinly. Lay the sugarpaste over the top of the cake and trim the edges. Decorate with orange and lemon rind.

Blueberry & Lemon Drizzle Cake

SERVES: 12

PREP: 20 MINS + 30 MINS COOLING

COOKING: 1 HR

Ingredients

8 oz/225 g butter, softened, plus extra for greasing

generous 1 cup golden superfine sugar

4 eggs, beaten

1¾ cups self-rising flour, sifted

finely grated rind and juice of 1 lemon

generous ¼ cup ground almonds

7 oz/200 g fresh blueberries

TOPPING

juice of 2 lemons

generous ½ cup golden superfine sugar

Preheat the oven to 350°F/180°C, then grease and line the bottom of an 8-inch/20-cm square cake pan. Place the butter and sugar in a bowl and beat together until light and fluffy. Gradually beat in the eggs, adding a little flour toward the end to prevent curdling. Beat in the lemon rind, then fold in the remaining flour and almonds with enough of the lemon juice to give a good dropping consistency.

Fold in three-quarters of the blueberries and turn into the prepared pan. Smooth the surface, then scatter the remaining blueberries on top. Bake in the preheated oven for 1 hour, or until firm to the touch and a skewer inserted into the center comes out clean.

To make the topping, place the lemon juice and sugar in a bowl and mix together. As soon as the cake comes out of the oven, prick it all over with a fine skewer and pour over the lemon mixture. Let cool in the pan until completely cold, then cut into 12 squares to serve.

Almond & Hazelnut Gâteau

SERVES: 8

PREP: 1 HR +
1 HR 40 MINS
COOLING/
CHILLING

COOKING: 25 MINS

Ingredients

butter, for greasing

4 eggs

½ cup superfine sugar

½ cup ground almonds

½ cup ground hazelnuts

5½ tbsp all-purpose flour

scant ½ cup slivered almonds

confectioners' sugar, for dusting

FILLING

3½ oz/100 g semisweet chocolate

1 tbsp butter

1¼ cups heavy cream

Preheat the oven to 375°F/190°C. Grease and line the bottoms of 2 x 7-inch/18-cm round sandwich cake pans.

Whisk the eggs and superfine sugar together for 10 minutes, or until light and foamy and the whisk leaves a trail that lasts a few seconds when lifted.

Fold in the ground almonds and hazelnuts, sift the flour and fold in with a metal spoon or spatula. Pour into the prepared pans.

Sprinkle the slivered almonds over the top of one of the cakes, then bake both cakes in the preheated oven for 15-20 minutes, or until springy to the touch.

Let cool in the pans for 5 minutes, then turn out onto wire racks to cool completely.

To make the filling, melt the chocolate, remove from the heat, and stir in the butter. Let cool. Whip the cream until holding its shape, then fold in the chocolate until mixed.

Place the cake without the extra almonds on a serving plate and spread the filling over it. Let set slightly, then place the almond-topped cake on top of the filling and let chill in the refrigerator for 1 hour. Dust with confectioners' sugar and serve.

Traditional Apple Pie

Ingredients

1 lb 10 oz-2 lb 4 oz/750 g-1 kg cooking apples, peeled, cored and sliced

generous ½ cup soft light brown or caster sugar, plus extra for sprinkling

½-1 tsp ground cinnamon, apple spice or ground ginger

1-2 tbsp water

PASTRY

3 cups all purpose flour

pinch of salt

6 tbsp butter or margarine

⅓ cup shortening

about 6 tbsp cold water

beaten egg or milk, for glazing

To make the pie dough, sift the flour and salt into a mixing bowl. Add the butter and fat and rub in with the fingertips until the mixture resembles fine breadcrumbs. Add the water and gather the mixture together into a dough. Wrap the dough and leave to chill for 30 minutes.

Preheat the oven to 220°C/425°F/Gas Mark 7. Roll out almost two-thirds of the pastry thinly and use to line a 20-23-cm/8-9-inch deep pie plate or shallow pie pan.

Mix the apples with the sugar and spice and pack into the pie shell; the filling can come up above the rim. Add the water if liked, particularly if the apples are a dry variety.

Roll out the remaining pie dough to form a lid. Dampen the edges of the pie rim with water and position the lid, pressing the edges firmly together. Trim and crimp the edges.

Use the trimmings to cut out leaves or other shapes to decorate the top of the pie, dampen and attach. Glaze the top of the pie with beaten egg or milk, make 1-2 slits in the top and put the pie on a cookie sheet.

Bake in the preheated oven for 20 minutes, then reduce the temperature to 180°C/350°F/Gas Mark 4 and cook for about 30 minutes, until the pastry is a light golden brown. Serve hot or cold, sprinkled with sugar.

Apple & Blackberry Crumble

2 lb/900 g tart cooking apples, peeled and sliced

10½ oz/300 g blackberries, fresh or frozen

¼ cup brown sugar

1 tsp ground cinnamon

custard or pouring cream, to serve

CRUMBLE

⅔ cup self-rising flour

⅔ cup whole-wheat all-purpose flour

4 oz/115 g butter

¼ cup raw brown sugar

Preheat the oven to 400°F/200°C. Peel and core the apples and cut into chunks. Place in a bowl with the blackberries, sugar, and cinnamon and mix together, then transfer to an ovenproof baking dish.

To make the crumble, sift the self-rising flour into a bowl and stir in the whole-wheat flour. Add the butter and rub it in with your fingers until the mixture resembles coarse bread crumbs. Stir in the sugar.

Spread the crumble over the apples and bake in the preheated oven for 40-45 minutes, or until the apples are soft and the crumble is golden brown and crisp. Serve with custard or pouring cream.

Sticky Toffee Sponge

Ingredients

SPONGE

scant ½ cup golden raisins

generous ¾ cup stoned dates, chopped

1 tsp baking soda

2 tbsp butter, plus extra for greasing

1 cup brown sugar

2 eggs

scant 1½ cups self-rising flour, sifted

STICKY TOFFEE SAUCE

2 tbsp butter

¾ cup heavy cream

1 cup brown sugar

grated orange zest, to decorate

freshly whipped cream, to serve

To make the sponge, put the fruits and baking soda into a heatproof bowl. Cover with boiling water and set aside to soak.

Preheat the oven to 350°F/180°C. Grease a round cake pan, 8 inches/20 cm in diameter, with butter. Put the remaining butter in a separate bowl, add the sugar, and mix well. Beat in the eggs then fold in the flour. Drain the soaked fruits, add to the bowl, and mix. Spoon the mixture evenly into the prepared cake pan. Transfer to the preheated oven and bake for 35-40 minutes. The sponge is cooked when a skewer inserted into the center comes out clean. About 5 minutes before the end of the cooking time, make the sauce. Melt the butter in a pan over medium heat. Stir in the cream and sugar and bring to a boil, stirring constantly. Lower the heat and simmer for 5 minutes.

Turn out the sponge onto a serving plate and pour over the sauce. Decorate with grated orange zest and serve with whipped cream.

Roly Poly Pudding

SERVES: 4

PREP: 20 MINS

COOKING: 1 HR 30 MINS

Ingredients

1¼ cups self-rising flour, plus
  extra for dusting

pinch of salt

2¾ oz/75 g shredded suet

3-4 tbsp hot water

6 tbsp raspberry preserve

2 tbsp milk

1 tbsp butter, for greasing

raspberries, to decorate

custard, to serve

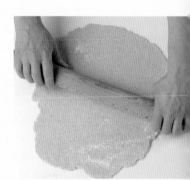

Put the flour and salt into a bowl and mix together well. Add the suet, then stir in enough hot water to make a light dough. Using your hands, shape the dough into a ball. Turn out the dough onto a lightly floured counter and knead gently until smooth. Roll out into a rectangle about 11 inches/28 cm x 9 inches/23 cm.

Spread the raspberry preserve over the dough, leaving a border of about ½ inch/1 cm all round. Brush the border with milk. Starting with the short side, roll up the dough evenly into one large roll.

Lightly grease a large piece of aluminum foil with butter, then place the dough roll in the center. Gently close up the foil around the dough, allowing room for expansion, and seal tightly. Transfer to a steamer on top of a pan of boiling water. Steam for about 1½ hours until cooked, topping up the water level when necessary.

Turn out the roly poly onto a serving platter and decorate with raspberries. Serve with hot custard.

Lemon Meringue Pie

Ingredients

PIE DOUGH

*scant 1½ cups all-purpose flour,
   plus extra for dusting*

*scant ½ cup butter, diced, plus
   extra for greasing*

*scant ½ cup confectioner's sugar,
   sifted*

finely grated zest of 1 lemon

1 egg yolk, beaten

3 tbsp milk

FILLING

3 tbsp cornstarch

1¼ cups cold water

juice and grated zest of 2 lemons

scant 1 cup superfine sugar

2 eggs, separated

To make the pie dough, sift the flour into a bowl and rub in the butter. Mix in the remaining ingredients. Knead briefly on a lightly floured counter. Let rest for 30 minutes. Preheat the oven to 350°F/180°C. Grease an 8-inch/20-cm ovenproof pie dish with butter. Roll out the dough to a thickness of ¼ inch/5 mm and use it to line the dish. Prick with a fork, line with baking parchment, and fill with baking beans. Bake for 15 minutes. Remove from the oven. Lower the temperature to 300°F/150°C.

To make the filling, mix the cornstarch with a little water. Put the remaining water into a pan. Stir in the lemon juice and zest and cornstarch paste. Bring to a boil, stirring. Cook for 2 minutes. Cool a little. Stir in 5 tablespoons of sugar and the egg yolks, and pour into the tart shell. In a separate bowl, whisk the egg whites until stiff. Gradually whisk in the remaining sugar and spread over the pie. Bake for 40 minutes. Remove from the oven and serve.

Bakewell Tart

SERVES: 4

PREP: 20 MINS + 30 MINS RESTING

COOKING: 40 MINS

Ingredients

PIE DOUGH

scant 1½ cups all-purpose flour, plus extra for dusting

scant ½ cup butter, diced, plus extra for greasing

scant ½ cup confectioner's sugar, sifted

finely grated zest of 1 lemon

1 egg yolk, beaten

3 tbsp milk

4 tbsp strawberry preserve

FILLING

scant ½ cup butter

½ cup brown sugar

2 eggs, beaten

1 tsp almond extract

75 g/2¾ oz ground rice

3 tbsp ground almonds

3 tbsp slivered almonds, toasted

confectioner's sugar, to dust

To make the pie dough, sift the flour into a bowl. Rub in the butter. Mix in the confectioner's sugar, lemon zest, egg yolk, and milk. Knead briefly on a lightly floured counter. Let rest for 30 minutes.

Preheat the oven to 375°F/190°C. Grease an 8-inch/20-cm ovenproof tart pan with butter. Roll out the dough to a thickness of ¼ inch/5 mm and use it to line the bottom and sides of the pan. Prick all over the bottom with a fork, then spread with preserve.

To make the filling, cream together the butter and sugar until fluffy. Gradually beat in the eggs, followed by the almond extract, ground rice, and ground almonds. Spread the mixture evenly over the preserve-covered tart shell, then scatter over the slivered almonds. Bake in the preheated oven for 40 minutes, until golden. Remove from the oven, dust with confectioner's sugar, and serve.

Dried Cherry Cheesecake Muffins

MAKES: 12

PREP: 15 MINS

COOKING: 12-15 MINS

5½ oz/150 g butter, plus extra
   for greasing

scant 1 cup cream cheese

generous ¾ cup superfine sugar

3 large eggs, lightly beaten

2 cups self-rising flour

generous ½ cup dried cherries,
   chopped

confectioners' sugar, for dusting

Preheat the oven to 350°F/180°C. Grease a deep 12-cup muffin pan.

Melt the butter and let cool slightly. In a large bowl, whisk the cream cheese and sugar together, add the eggs one at a time until well combined, and then stir in the melted butter.

Mix the flour and cherries together in a bowl, then stir gently into the batter. Spoon into the prepared muffin pan, filling each hole to about two-thirds full, and bake for 12-15 minutes, or until golden brown. Remove from the oven and let cool on a wire rack. Eat warm or cold, dusted lightly with confectioners' sugar.

MAKES:	11
PREP:	15 MINS
COOKING:	20 MINS

Triple Chocolate Muffins

Ingredients

1¾ cups all-purpose flour

¼ cup unsweetened cocoa

2 tsp baking powder

½ tsp baking soda

generous ½ cup semisweet
  chocolate chips

generous ½ cup white
  chocolate chips

2 eggs, beaten

1¼ cups sour cream

scant ½ cup brown sugar

6 tbsp butter, melted

Preheat the oven to 400°F/200°C. Line 11 holes of 1 or 2 muffin pans with paper muffin cases. Sift the flour, cocoa, baking powder, and baking soda into a large bowl, add the semisweet and white chocolate chips, and stir.

Place the eggs, sour cream, sugar, and butter in a separate bowl and mix. Add the wet ingredients to the dry ingredients and stir gently until just combined.

Using 2 forks, divide the batter between the paper cases and bake in the preheated oven for 20 minutes, or until well risen and firm to the touch. Serve warm or cold.

Apple & Cinnamon Muffins

MAKES: 6

PREP: 15 MINS

COOKING: 20-25 MINS

Ingredients

⅔ cup whole-wheat all-purpose flour

½ cup white all-purpose flour

1½ tsp baking powder

pinch of salt

1 tsp ground cinnamon

scant ¼ cup golden superfine sugar

2 small eating apples, peeled, cored, and finely chopped

½ cup milk

1 egg, beaten

2 oz/55 g butter, melted

TOPPING

12 brown sugar cubes, coarsely crushed

½ tsp ground cinnamon

Preheat the oven to 400°F/200°C. Line 6 holes of a muffin pan with paper muffin cases.

Sift the 2 flours, baking powder, salt, and cinnamon into a large bowl and stir in the sugar and chopped apples. Place the milk, egg, and butter in a separate bowl and mix. Add the wet ingredients to the dry ingredients and gently stir until just combined.

Divide the mixture between the paper cases. To make the topping, mix together the crushed sugar cubes and cinnamon and sprinkle over the muffins. Bake in the preheated oven for 20-25 minutes, or until risen and golden. Serve the muffins warm or cold.

Classic Oatmeal Cookies

MAKES: 30

PREP: 10 MINS

COOKING: 15 MINS

Ingredients

¾ cup butter or margarine, plus extra for greasing

scant 1⅓ cups raw brown sugar

1 egg

4 tbsp water

1 tsp vanilla extract

4⅓ cups rolled oats

1 cup all-purpose flour

1 tsp salt

½ tsp baking soda

Preheat the oven to 350°F/180°C and grease a large cookie sheet.

Cream the butter (or margarine, if using) and sugar together in a large mixing bowl. Beat in the egg, water, and vanilla extract until the mixture is smooth.

In a separate bowl, mix the oats, flour, salt, and baking soda. Gradually stir the oat mixture into the butter mixture until thoroughly combined.

Put 30 rounded tablespoonfuls of cookie mixture onto the greased cookie sheet, making sure they are well spaced. Transfer to the preheated oven and bake for 15 minutes, or until the cookies are golden brown.

Remove the cookies from the oven and place on a wire rack to cool before serving.

Peanut Butter Cookies

Ingredients

*4 oz /115 g butter, softened, plus
  extra for greasing*

scant ½ cup crunchy peanut butter

*generous ½ cup golden superfine
  sugar*

generous ½ cup brown sugar

1 egg, beaten

½ tsp vanilla extract

⅔ cup all-purpose flour

½ tsp baking soda

½ tsp baking powder

pinch of salt

1½ cups rolled oats

Preheat the oven to 350°F/180°C, then grease
3 cookie sheets. Place the butter and peanut butter
in a bowl and beat together. Beat in the superfine and
brown sugars, then gradually beat in the egg and
vanilla extract.

Sift the flour, baking soda, baking powder, and salt
into the bowl and stir in the oats. Drop spoonfuls of
the cookie dough onto the cookie sheets, spaced
well apart to allow for spreading. Flatten slightly
with a fork.

Bake in the preheated oven for 12 minutes, or
until lightly browned. Let cool on the cookie sheets
for 2 minutes, then transfer to wire racks to cool
completely.

Cherry & Walnut Cookies

Ingredients

¾ cup butter or margarine,
   plus extra for greasing

1 cup soft brown sugar

2 eggs

2¼ cups all-purpose flour

pinch of salt

2 tsp baking powder

2 tbsp milk

1 tsp almond extract

1 cup chopped walnuts

½ cup raisins

scant ½ cup golden raisins

½ cup maraschino cherries

2 cups wheat flakes, crushed

15 maraschino cherries, cut in half
(optional)

Preheat the oven to 375°F/190°C. Grease a large cookie sheet, cut the cherries in half.

Cream the butter and sugar in a large mixing bowl until a fluffy consistency is reached. Beat in the eggs.

Gradually sift the flour, salt, and baking powder into the creamed mixture. Add the milk and almond extract and mix thoroughly. Stir in the walnuts and dried fruit and mix well.

Form the dough into 30 balls (about 1 rounded tablespoon each) and roll in the crushed wheat flakes. Space the dough balls about 1 inch/2 cm apart on the greased cookie sheet. Place half a maraschino cherry on the top of each dough ball, if desired. Transfer to the preheated oven and cook for 10 minutes, or until the cookies are light brown.

Transfer from the oven to a wire rack and let them cool.

Gingersnaps

Ingredients

½ cup butter, plus extra for
  greasing

2½ cups self-rising flour

pinch of salt

1 cup superfine sugar

1 tbsp ground ginger

1 tsp baking soda

¼ cup light corn syrup

1 egg, lightly beaten

1 tsp grated orange zest

 with a little butter

Lightly grease several cookie sheets.

Strain the flour, salt, sugar, ground ginger, and baking
soda into a large mixing bowl.

Heat the butter and light corn syrup together in a pan
over very low heat until the butter has melted.

Let the butter mixture cool slightly, then pour it onto
the dry ingredients. Add the egg and orange zest and
mix together thoroughly.

Using your hands, carefully shape the dough into
30 even-size balls.

Place the balls well apart on the prepared cookie
sheets, then flatten them slightly with your fingers.

Bake in a preheated oven, 325°F/160°C, for
15-20 minutes.

Carefully transfer the cookies to a wire rack to cool
and crispen.

Chocolate Drop Cookies

MAKES: 20

PREP: 10 MINS

COOKING: 15-20 MINS

Ingredients

4 oz/115 g butter, plus extra
 for greasing

⅔ cup all-purpose flour

2 tbsp unsweetened cocoa

¼ cup superfine sugar

½ tsp vanilla extract

Preheat the oven to 375°F/190°C. Grease 2-3 large cookie sheets. Sift the flour and cocoa together.

Whisk the butter, superfine sugar, and vanilla extract together in a large bowl until soft and fluffy. Stir in the flour mixture until well blended.

Drop teaspoonfuls of the mixture on to the prepared cookie sheets, allowing room for the cookies to spread during cooking.

Bake the cookies in the preheated oven for 15-20 minutes, until firm. Leave for 1 minute, then transfer to a wire rack and let cool.

Gingerbread People

MAKES: 20, USING LARGE CUTTERS

PREP: 30 MINS + 30 MINS COOLING

COOKING: 15-20 MINS

Ingredients

½ cup butter, plus extra
  for greasing

3½ cups all-purpose flour,
  plus extra for dusting

2 tsp ground ginger

1 tsp allspice

2 tsp baking soda

generous ⅓ cup corn syrup

generous ½ cup brown sugar

1 egg, beaten

TO DECORATE

currants

candied cherries

generous ¾ cup confectioners'
  sugar

3-4 tsp water

Preheat the oven to 325°F/160°C, then grease 3 large cookie sheets. Sift the flour, ginger, allspice, and baking soda into a large bowl. Place the butter, syrup, and sugar in a pan over low heat and stir until melted. Pour onto the dry ingredients and add the egg. Mix together to form a dough. The dough will be sticky to start with, but will become firmer as it cools.

On a lightly floured counter, roll out the dough to about ⅛-inch/3-mm thick and stamp out gingerbread people shapes. Place on the prepared cookie sheets. Re-knead and re-roll the trimmings and cut out more shapes until the dough is used up. Decorate with currants for eyes and pieces of cherry for mouths. Bake in the oven for 15-20 minutes, or until firm and lightly browned.

Remove from the oven and let cool on the cookie sheets for a few minutes, then transfer to wire racks to cool completely. Mix the confectioners' sugar with the water to a thick consistency. Place the frosting in a small plastic bag and cut a tiny hole in one corner. Use the frosting to draw buttons or clothes shapes on the cooled cookies.

Lemon Butterfly Cakes

MAKES: 12

PREP: 20 MINS +
30 MINS
COOLING

COOKING: 15-20 MINS

Ingredients

generous ¾ cup self-rising flour

½ tsp baking powder

4 oz/115 g butter, softened

generous ½ cup golden superfine sugar

2 eggs, beaten

finely grated rind of ½ lemon

2-4 tbsp milk

confectioners' sugar, for dusting

filling

¼ cup butter

generous 1 cup confectioners' sugar

1 tbsp lemon juice

Preheat the oven to 375°F/190°C. Place 12 paper cases in a muffin pan. Sift the flour and baking powder into a bowl. Add the butter, sugar, eggs, lemon rind, and enough milk to give a medium-soft consistency. Beat thoroughly until smooth. Divide the batter between the paper cases and bake in the preheated oven for 15-20 minutes, or until well risen and golden. Transfer to wire racks to cool.

To make the filling, place the butter in a bowl, then sift in the confectioners' sugar and add the lemon juice. Beat well until smooth and creamy. When the cakes are quite cold, use a sharp-pointed vegetable knife to cut a circle from the top of each cake, then cut each circle in half.

Spoon a little of the buttercream into the center of each cake and press the 2 semi-circular pieces into it to resemble wings. Dust the cakes with sifted confectioners' sugar before serving.

Fruity Flapjacks

Ingredients

sunflower or corn oil, for brushing

1¼ cups rolled oats

¾ cup raw sugar

½ cup raisins

4 oz/115 g lowfat sunflower margarine, melted

Preheat the oven to 375°F/190°C. Lightly brush an 11 x 7-inch/28 x 18-cm shallow rectangular cake pan with oil. Combine the oats, sugar, and raisins with the margarine, stirring well.

Spoon the oat mixture into the pan and press down firmly with the back of a spoon. Bake in the preheated oven for 15-20 minutes, or until golden.

Using a sharp knife, score lines to mark out 14 bars, then let the flapjack cool in the pan for 10 minutes. Carefully transfer the bars to a wire rack to cool completely.

Chocolate Chip Flapjacks

MAKES: 12

PREP: 40 MINS

COOKING: 40 MINS

Ingredients

*4 oz/115 g butter, plus extra
 for greasing*

⅓ cup superfine sugar

1 tbsp corn syrup

4 cups rolled oats

½ cup semisweet chocolate chips

⅓ cup golden raisins

Preheat the oven to 350°F/180°C. Lightly grease a shallow 8-inch/20-cm square cake pan.

Place the butter, superfine sugar, and corn syrup in a pan and cook over low heat, stirring constantly until the butter and sugar melt and the mixture is well combined.

Remove the pan from the heat and stir in the rolled oats until they are well coated. Add the chocolate chips and the golden raisins and mix well to combine everything.

Turn into the prepared pan and press down well.

Bake in the preheated oven for 30 minutes. Cool slightly, then mark into fingers. When almost cold cut into bars or squares and transfer to a wire rack to cool completely.

Double Chocolate Brownies

Ingredients

4 oz/115 g butter, plus extra for greasing

4 oz/115 g semisweet chocolate, broken into pieces

1⅓ cups golden superfine sugar

pinch of salt

1 tsp vanilla extract

2 large eggs

1 cup all-purpose flour

2 tbsp unsweetened cocoa

½ cup white chocolate chips

FUDGE SAUCE

4 tbsp butter

generous 1 cup golden superfine sugar

⅔ cup milk

generous 1 cup heavy cream

⅔ cup corn syrup

7 oz/200 g semisweet chocolate, broken into pieces

Preheat the oven to 350°F/180°C. Grease and line the bottom of a 7-inch/18-cm square cake pan. Place the butter and chocolate in a small heatproof bowl set over a saucepan of gently simmering water until melted. Stir until smooth. Let cool slightly. Stir in the sugar, salt, and vanilla extract. Add the eggs, one at a time, stirring well, until blended.

Sift the flour and unsweetened cocoa into the cake batter and beat until smooth. Stir in the chocolate chips, then pour the batter into the pan. Bake in the preheated oven for 35-40 minutes, or until the top is evenly colored and a toothpick inserted into the center comes out almost clean. Let cool slightly while preparing the sauce.

To make the sauce, place the butter, sugar, milk, cream, and syrup in a small saucepan and heat gently until the sugar has dissolved. Bring to a boil and stir for 10 minutes, or until the mixture is caramel-colored. Remove from the heat and add the chocolate. Stir until smooth. Cut the brownies into squares and serve immediately with the sauce.

Hazelnut Squares

Ingredients

*3½ oz/100 g butter, cut into small
pieces, plus extra for greasing*

generous 1 cup all-purpose flour

salt

1 tsp baking powder

*generous ¾ cup firmly packed
brown sugar*

1 egg, beaten

4 tbsp milk

generous ¾ cup hazelnuts, halved

*raw brown sugar, for sprinkling
(optional)*

Preheat the oven to 350°F/180°C. Grease a 9-inch/
23-cm square cake pan and line the bottom with
parchment paper. Sift the flour, a pinch of salt and the
baking powder into a large bowl. Add the butter and
rub it in with your fingertips until the mixture
resembles fine bread crumbs. Add the brown sugar
and stir to mix.

Add the egg, milk, and halved hazelnuts to the dry
ingredients and stir well until thoroughly combined
and the cookie dough is a soft consistency.

Spoon the cookie dough into the cake pan and smooth
the surface. Sprinkle with raw brown sugar (if using).
Bake in the oven for 25 minutes, or until it is firm to
the touch when pressed with a finger. Let cool in the
pan for 10 minutes, then loosen the edges with a
round-bladed knife and turn out onto a wire rack to
cool completely. Cut into squares.

Cappuccino Squares

Ingredients

8 oz/225 g butter, softened, plus extra for greasing

generous 1½ cups self-rising flour

1 tsp baking powder

1 tsp unsweetened cocoa, plus extra for dusting

generous 1 cup golden superfine sugar

4 eggs, beaten

3 tbsp instant coffee powder dissolved in 2 tbsp hot water

FROSTING

4 oz/115 g white chocolate, broken into pieces

4 tbsp butter, softened

3 tbsp milk

1¾ cups confectioners' sugar

unsweetened cocoa, to decorate

Preheat the oven to 350°F/180°C. Grease and line the bottom of a shallow oblong 11 x 7-inch/28 x 18-cm pan. Sift the flour, baking powder, and unsweetened cocoa into a bowl and add the butter, superfine sugar, eggs, and coffee. Beat well, by hand or with an electric whisk, until smooth, then spoon into the pan and smooth the top.

Bake in the oven for 35-40 minutes, or until risen and firm. Let cool in the pan for 10 minutes, then turn out on to a wire rack and peel off the lining paper. Let cool completely. To make the frosting, place the chocolate, butter, and milk in a bowl set over a pan of simmering water and stir until the chocolate has melted.

Remove the bowl from the pan and sift in the confectioners' sugar. Beat until smooth, then spread over the cake. Dust the top of the cake with sifted cocoa, then cut into squares.

Sweet Delights

Had a bad day and need something to cheer you up?

Had a good day and feel like celebrating? Either way, you need look no

farther as this chapter is packed with delectable treats to provide comfort

or add sparkle. Recipes for tarts and pies, little cakes and rich desserts,

bars, and cookies all vie with each other to tempt your taste buds, satisfy

your sweet tooth, and make every day seem special. They are ideal too for

home-baked gifts–always a joy to receive–or for that most competitive

of activities, the school cake sale. You don't have to be an expert to create

the simple elegance of Tarte au Citron (see page 58), the self-indulgent

luxury of Chocolate Fudge Cake (see page 74), the satisfying stickiness of

Chelsea Buns (see page 77),or the scrumptiousness of

Chewy Golden Cookies (see page 90).

Go on, spoil yourself!

Tarte Au Citron

Ingredients

butter, for greasing

all-purpose flour, for dusting

1 quantity Pâte Sucrée

FILLING

1 large egg

4 large egg yolks

scant ¾ cup golden superfine sugar

*finely grated rind and juice of
  4 lemons (the juice should
  measure ⅔ cup)*

⅔ cup heavy cream

confectioners' sugar, for dusting

Preheat the oven to 400°F/200°C, then grease a 9-inch/23-cm tart pan. On a lightly floured counter, roll out the pastry and use it to line the tart pan, then bake blind. Reduce the oven temperature to 325°F/160C and place a cookie sheet in the oven.

To make the filling, place the egg, egg yolks, and sugar in a bowl and whisk until smooth. Gently stir in the lemon rind, lemon juice, and cream. Pour most of the filling into the tart shell, then place the tart pan on the preheated cookie sheet in the oven and spoon in the rest of the filling.

Bake in the oven for 25-30 minutes, or until there is no sign of liquid movement in the filling. Let cool in the pan for 15 minutes and serve warm or chilled. Before serving, sift over the confectioners' sugar to dust.

SERVES: 6

PREP: 20 MINS +
           15 MINS
           COOLING

COOKING: 40-55 MINS

SERVES: 4

PREP: 20 MINS +
1 HR 15 MINS
REST/COOL

COOKING: 15 MINS

Peach & Strawberry Tart

Ingredients

PIE DOUGH

scant 1½ cups all-purpose flour,
plus extra for dusting

scant ½ cup butter, diced, plus
extra for greasing

scant ½ cup confectioner's sugar,
sifted

finely grated zest of 1 orange

1 egg yolk, beaten

3 tbsp milk

FILLING

¾ cup heavy cream

4 tbsp confectioner's sugar

1 tbsp peach liqueur

4 tbsp strawberry preserve

2 peaches, pitted and sliced

3½ oz/100 g strawberries, hulled
and sliced

confectioner's sugar, to dust

whipped cream, to serve

To make the dough, sift the flour into a bowl. Rub in the butter, then mix in the sugar, orange zest, egg yolk, and milk. Knead briefly on a lightly floured counter, then let rest for 30 minutes. Preheat the oven to 350°F/180°C. Grease a 9-inch/23-cm tart pan with butter. Roll out the dough to a thickness of ¼ inch/ 5 mm and use to line the bottom and sides of the tin. Prick the bottom with a fork, line with baking parchment, and fill with baking beans. Bake for 15 minutes. Remove from the oven and set aside.

To make the filling, put the cream into a bowl and beat in the confectioner's sugar. Stir in the peach liqueur. Spread the bottom of the pastry shell with strawberry preserve, then spoon in the cream filling. Arrange the sliced peaches and strawberries over the top, then cover with plastic wrap and refrigerate for 45 minutes. Remove from the refrigerator, dust with confectioner's sugar, and serve with whipped cream.

Blueberry Clafoutis

SERVES: 4

PREP: 15 MINS

COOKING: 30 MINS

Ingredients

2 tbsp butter, plus extra
for greasing

scant ⅔ cup superfine sugar

3 eggs

scant ½ cup all-purpose flour

generous 1 cup light cream

½ tsp ground cinnamon

1 lb/450 g blueberries

confectioner's sugar, to dust

light cream, to serve

Preheat the oven to 350°F/180°C. Grease a 4-cup ovenproof dish with butter.

Put the remaining butter into a bowl with the sugar, and cream together until fluffy. Add the eggs and beat together well. Mix in the flour, then gradually stir in the cream, followed by the cinnamon. Continue to stir until smooth.

Arrange the blueberries evenly across the bottom of the prepared dish, then pour over the cream batter. Transfer to the preheated oven and bake for about 30 minutes, or until puffed and golden. Remove from the oven, dust with confectioner's sugar, and serve with light cream.

Forest Fruit Pie

Ingredients

9 oz/250 g blueberries

9 oz/250 g raspberries

9 oz/250 g blackberries

½ cup superfine sugar

scant 1½ cups all-purpose flour,
plus extra for dusting

scant ¼ cup ground hazelnuts

scant ½ cup butter, diced, plus
extra for greasing

finely grated zest of 1 lemon

1 egg yolk, beaten

4 tbsp milk

2 tsp confectioner's sugar, to dust

whipped cream, to serve

Put the fruit into a pan with 3 tablespoons of superfine sugar and simmer, stirring, for 5 minutes. Remove from the heat. Sift the flour into a bowl, then add the hazelnuts. Rub in the butter, then sift in the remaining sugar. Add the lemon zest, egg yolk, and 3 tablespoons of milk, and mix. Turn out onto a lightly floured counter and knead briefly. Let rest for 30 minutes.

Preheat the oven to 375°F/190°C. Grease an 8-inch/20-cm ovenproof pie dish with butter. Roll out half the dough to a thickness of ¼ inch/5 mm and use it to line the dish. Spoon the fruit into the pie shell. Brush the rim with water, then roll out the remaining dough and use it to cover the pie. Trim and crimp the edges, make 2 small slits in the top, and decorate with 2 leaf shapes cut from the dough trimmings. Brush all over with the remaining milk. Bake for 40 minutes. Remove from the oven, sprinkle over the confectioner's sugar, and serve with whipped cream.

Banoffee Pie

Ingredients

two cans sweetened condensed
  milk, about 14 fl oz/400 ml each

6 tbsp butter, melted

5½ oz/150 g graham crackers,
  crushed into crumbs

⅓ cup almonds, toasted
  and ground

⅓ cup hazelnuts, toasted
  and ground

4 ripe bananas

1 tbsp lemon juice

1 tsp vanilla extract

2¾ oz/75 g chocolate, grated

scant 2 cups thick heavy
  cream, whipped

SERVES: 4

PREP: 20 MINS +
           1 HR COOLING

COOKING: 2 HRS 15 MINS

Place the cans of milk in a large pan and cover them with water. Bring to a boil, then reduce the heat and simmer for 2 hours, topping up the water level regularly to keep the cans covered. Carefully lift out the hot cans and let cool.

Preheat the oven to 350°F/180°C. Grease a 9-inch/23-cm tart pan with butter. Put the remaining butter into a bowl and add the crackers and nuts. Mix together well, then press the mixture evenly into the bottom and sides of the tart pan. Bake for 10-12 minutes, then remove from the oven and let cool.

Peel and slice the bananas and put them into a bowl. Sprinkle over the lemon juice and vanilla extract and mix gently. Spread the banana mixture over the cracker layer in the pan, then open the cans of condensed milk and spoon the contents over the bananas. Sprinkle over 1¾ oz/50 g of the chocolate, then top with a thick layer of whipped cream. Scatter over the remaining chocolate and serve.

Manhattan Cheesecake

Ingredients

sunflower or corn oil, for brushing

6 tbsp butter

7 oz/200 g graham crackers, crushed

1¾ cups cream cheese

2 large eggs

scant ¾ cup superfine sugar

1½ tsp vanilla extract

scant 2 cups sour cream

BLUEBERRY TOPPING

¼ cup superfine sugar

4 tbsp water

9 oz/250 g fresh blueberries

1 tsp arrowroot

Preheat the oven to 375°F/190°C. Brush an 8-inch/20-cm springform pan with oil. Melt the butter in a pan over low heat. Stir in the crackers, then spread in the pan. Place the cream cheese, eggs, ½ cup of the sugar, and ½ teaspoon of the vanilla extract in a food processor. Process until smooth. Pour over the cracker layer and smooth the top. Place on a baking sheet and bake for 20 minutes, or until set. Remove from the oven and let stand for 20 minutes. Leave the oven switched on.

Mix the cream with the remaining sugar and vanilla extract in a bowl. Spoon over the cheesecake. Return it to the oven for 10 minutes, let cool, then chill in the refrigerator for 8 hours, or overnight.

To make the topping, place the sugar in a pan with half of the water over low heat and stir until the sugar has dissolved. Increase the heat, add the blueberries, cover, and cook for a few minutes, or until they start to soften. Remove from the heat. Mix the arrowroot and remaining water in a bowl, add to the fruit, and stir until smooth. Return to low heat. Cook until the juice thickens and turns translucent. Let cool. Remove the cheesecake from the pan 1 hour before serving. Spoon the fruit on top and chill until ready to serve.

SERVES: 8-10

PREP: 20 MINS + 10 HRS COOLING/CHILLING

COOKING: 35 MINS

Strawberry Roulade

SERVES: 8

PREP: 30 MINS

COOKING: 10 MINS

Ingredients

3 large eggs

⅔ cup superfine sugar

scant 1 cup all-purpose flour

1 tbsp hot water

FILLING

¾ cup low-fat mascarpone

1 tsp almond extract

1½ cups small strawberries

TO DECORATE

1 tbsp slivered almonds, toasted

1 tsp confectioners' sugar

a few strawberries

Line a 14 x 10 inch/35 x 25 cm jelly roll pan with baking parchment.

Place the eggs in a heatproof bowl with the superfine sugar. Place the bowl over a pan of hot water and whisk until pale and thick.

Remove the bowl from the pan. Strain in the flour and fold into the eggs along with the hot water. Pour the mixture into the pan and bake in a preheated oven, 425°F/220°C, for 8-10 minutes until golden and set.

Turn out the cake onto a sheet of baking parchment. Peel off the lining paper and roll up the sponge cake tightly along with the baking parchment. Wrap in a dish cloth and let cool.

Mix together the mascarpone and the almond extract. Reserving a few strawberries for decoration, wash, hull, and slice the rest. Chill mascarpone mixture and the strawberries in the refrigerator until required.

Unroll the cake, spread the mascarpone mixture over the surface, and sprinkle with sliced strawberries. Roll the cake up again and transfer to a serving plate. Sprinkle with almonds and lightly dust with confectioners' sugar. Decorate with the reserved strawberries.

69

Raspberry Dessert Cake

Ingredients

8 oz/225 g butter, plus extra for greasing

9 oz/250 g semisweet chocolate, broken into pieces

1 tbsp strong dark coffee

5 eggs

⅜ cup golden superfine sugar

¾ cup all-purpose flour

1 tsp ground cinnamon

¾ cup fresh raspberries

confectioners' sugar, for dusting

TO SERVE

fresh raspberries

whipped cream

Preheat the oven to 325°F/160°C. Grease a 9-inch/ 23-cm cake pan with butter and line the bottom with parchment paper. Place the chocolate, butter, and coffee in a small heatproof bowl and set over a pan of gently simmering water until melted. Stir and let cool slightly.

Place the eggs and sugar in a separate bowl and beat together until thick and pale. Gently fold in the chocolate cake batter. Sift the flour and ground cinnamon into a separate bowl, then fold into the chocolate cake batter. Pour into the pan and sprinkle the raspberries evenly over the top.

Bake in the oven for 35-45 minutes, or until the cake is well risen and springy to the touch. Let cool in the pan for 15 minutes before turning out onto a large serving plate. Dust with confectioners' sugar before serving with fresh raspberries and cream.

Chocolate Panforte

SERVES: 4-6

PREP: 20 MINS +
         1 HR COOLING

COOKING: 1 HR

Ingredients

½ cup chopped candied orange peel

8 dried apricots, chopped

2 tbsp orange-flavored liqueur, such as Cointreau

1 cup shelled whole hazelnuts

1 generous cup split almonds, toasted

⅞ cup all-purpose flour

2 tbsp unsweetened cocoa powder

2 tsp allspice

scant ¾ cup superfine sugar

5 tbsp clear honey

confectioners' sugar, to decorate

Preheat the oven to 300°F/150°C. Line an 8-inch/20-cm round cake pan.

Put the orange peel, apricots, and liqueur into a heatproof bowl and let soak. Toast the hazelnuts under a preheated medium broiler until the skins split, remove to a clean dish towel, and rub to remove the skins. Coarsely chop, then add to the fruit with the almonds and mix well. Sift the flour, cocoa powder, and allspice into a separate bowl, then mix into the fruit and nuts. Bring the sugar and honey to a boil in a pan over low heat, stirring. Continue to boil, stirring, for 5 minutes, then quickly pour the syrup over the fruit and mix well. Turn into the prepared pan and level the surface. Bake in the oven for 50 minutes.

Remove from the oven, turn out on to a wire rack, and discard the lining paper. Let cool, then dredge with confectioners' sugar. Serve immediately or store for up to 3-4 months in an airtight container.

Crème Brûlée Tarts

SERVES: 6

PREP: 2 HRS 20 MINS

COOKING: 25 MINS

Ingredients

SWEET PIE DOUGH

1¼ cups all-purpose flour

2 tbsp superfine sugar

½ cup butter, cut into small pieces.

1 tbsp water

FILLING

4 egg yolks

¼ cup superfine sugar

1¾ cups heavy cream

1 tsp vanilla extract

raw brown sugar, for sprinkling

To make the dough, place the flour and sugar in a bowl and rub in the butter with your fingertips until the mixture resembles bread crumbs. Add the water and work the mixture together until a soft dough has formed. Wrap and chill in the refrigerator for 30 minutes.

On a lightly floured surface, roll out the dough to line 6 tart pans, each 4 inches/10 cm wide. Prick the bottom of the tart shells with a fork and chill in the refrigerator for 20 minutes.

Line the tart shells with foil and baking beans and bake in a preheated oven, 375°F/190°C, for 15 minutes. Remove the foil and beans and cook for a further 10 minutes until crisp and golden. Let cool.

Meanwhile, make the filling. In a bowl, beat the egg yolks and sugar until pale. Heat the cream and vanilla extract in a pan until just below boiling point, then pour it onto the egg mixture, whisking constantly.

Return the mixture to a clean pan and bring to just below a boil, stirring constantly until thick. Do not let the mixture boil or it will curdle.

Let the mixture cool slightly, then pour it into the tart pans. Let cool and then chill overnight in the refrigerator.

Sprinkle the tarts with the sugar. Place under a preheated hot broiler for a few minutes. Let cool, then chill for 2 hours before serving.

Chocolate Fudge Cake

SERVES: 8

PREP: 25 MINS +
2 HRS
COOLING/
CHILLING

COOKING: 35-45 MINS

Ingredients

6 oz/175 g unsalted butter,
 softened, plus extra for greasing

generous 1 cup golden
 superfine sugar

3 eggs, beaten

3 tbsp corn syrup

3 tbsp ground almonds

generous 1 cup self-rising flour

pinch of salt

¼ cup unsweetened cocoa

FROSTING

8 oz/225 g semisweet chocolate,
 broken into pieces

¼ cup dark brown sugar

8 oz/225 g unsalted butter, diced

5 tbsp evaporated milk

½ tsp vanilla extract

Grease and line the bottom of 2 x 8-inch/20-cm cake pans. To make the frosting, place the chocolate, sugar, butter, evaporated milk, and vanilla extract in a heavy-bottom pan. Heat gently, stirring constantly, until melted. Pour into a bowl and let cool. Cover and let chill in the refrigerator for 1 hour, or until spreadable.

Preheat the oven to 350°F/180°C. Place the butter and sugar in a bowl and beat together until light and fluffy. Gradually beat in the eggs. Stir in the syrup and ground almonds. Sift the flour, salt, and unsweetened cocoa into a separate bowl, then fold into the cake batter. Add a little water, if necessary, to make a dropping consistency. Spoon the cake batter into the prepared pans and bake in the oven for 30-35 minutes, or until springy to the touch and the tip of a knife inserted in the center comes out clean.

Let stand in the pans for 5 minutes, then turn out onto wire racks to cool completely. When the cakes are cold, sandwich them together with half the frosting. Spread the remaining frosting over the top and sides of the cake, swirling it to give a frosted appearance.

SERVES: 8

PREP: 10 MINS

COOKING: 10 MINS

Cherry Biscuits

Ingredients

6 tbsp butter, cut into small pieces, plus extra for greasing

1½ cups self-rising flour

1-2 tsp superfine sugar

pinch of salt

¼ cup candied cherries, chopped

¼ cup golden raisins

1 egg, beaten

¼ cup milk

all-purpose flour, for dusting

Preheat the oven to 425°F/220°C. Lightly grease a cookie sheet with a little butter. Sift the flour, sugar, and salt into a large bowl. Add the butter and rub it in with your fingertips until the mixture resembles bread crumbs. Stir in the candied cherries and golden raisins. Add the egg. Set aside 1 tablespoon of the milk for glazing, then add the remainder to the mixture. Mix together to form a soft dough.

On a lightly floured counter, roll out the dough to a thickness of ¾ inch/2 cm and cut out 8 biscuits, using a 2-inch/5-cm cutter. Place the biscuits on the cookie sheet and brush the tops with the reserved milk.

Bake in the preheated oven for 8-10 minutes, or until the biscuits are golden brown. Let cool on a wire rack, then serve split and buttered, if you like.

Chelsea Buns

MAKES: 9

PREP: 30 MINS +
1 HR 45 MINS
RISING

COOKING: 30 MINS

Ingredients

2 tbsp butter, plus extra
  for greasing

generous 1½ cups strong white
  bread flour, plus extra for dusting

½ tsp salt

2 tsp active dry yeast

1 tsp golden superfine sugar

½ cup tepid milk

1 egg, beaten

vegetable oil, for brushing

generous ¾ cup confectioners'
  sugar, to glaze

FILLING

¼ cup brown sugar

4 oz/115 g luxury mixed dry fruit

1 tsp ground allspice

2 oz/55 g butter, softened

Grease a 7-inch/18-cm square cake pan. Sift the flour and salt into a warmed bowl, stir in the yeast and sugar, and rub in the butter. Make a well in the center. In a separate bowl, mix the milk and egg and pour into the dry ingredients. Beat to make a soft dough. Turn out onto a floured counter and knead for 5-10 minutes, or until smooth. Brush a clean bowl with oil, place the dough in the bowl, cover with plastic wrap and let stand in a warm place for 1 hour, or until doubled in size.

Turn the dough out onto a floured counter and knead lightly for 1 minute. Roll out into a 12 x 9-inch/30 x 23-cm rectangle.

To make the filling, place the brown sugar, fruit, and spice in a bowl and mix. Spread the dough with the softened butter and sprinkle the fruit mixture on top. Roll up from a long side, then cut into 9 pieces. Place in the prepared pan, cut-side up. Cover with oiled plastic wrap and let stand in a warm place for 45 minutes, or until risen.

Preheat the oven to 375°F/190°C. Bake the buns in the oven for 30 minutes, or until golden. Let cool in the pan for 10 minutes, then transfer, in one piece, to a wire rack to cool. Sift the confectioners' sugar into a bowl and stir in enough water to make a thin glaze. Brush over the buns and let set. Pull the buns apart to serve.

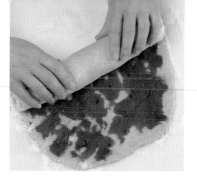

MAKES: 8

PREP: 20 MINS

COOKING: 35 MINS

Simple Cinnamon Rolls

Ingredients

scant 2½ cups self-rising flour

pinch of salt

2 tbsp superfine sugar

1 tsp ground cinnamon

3½ oz/100 g butter, melted, plus extra for greasing

2 egg yolks

scant 1 cup milk, plus extra for glazing

FILLING

1 tsp ground cinnamon

generous ¼ cup brown sugar

2 tbsp superfine sugar

1 tbsp butter, melted

FROSTING

generous 1 cup confectioners' sugar, sifted

2 tbsp cream cheese, softened

1 tbsp butter, softened

about 2 tbsp boiling water

1 tsp vanilla extract

Preheat the oven to 350°F/180°C. Grease an 8-inch/20-cm round pan and line the bottom with parchment paper.

Mix the flour, salt, superfine sugar, and cinnamon together in a bowl. Whisk the butter, egg yolks, and milk together and combine with the dry ingredients to make a soft dough. Turn out onto a large piece of waxed paper, lightly sprinkled with flour, and roll out to a rectangle 12 x 10 inches/30 x 25 cm.

To make the filling, mix the ingredients together, spread evenly over the dough and roll up, jelly-roll style, to form a log. Using a sharp knife, cut the dough into 8 even-size slices and pack into the prepared pan. Brush gently with extra milk and bake for 30-35 minutes, or until golden brown. Remove from the oven and let cool for 5 minutes before removing from the pan.

Sift the confectioners' sugar into a large bowl and make a well in the center. Place the cream cheese and butter in the center, pour over the water, and stir to mix. Add extra boiling water, a few drops at a time, until the frosting coats the back of a spoon. Stir in the vanilla extract. Drizzle over the rolls. Serve warm or cold.

Apple Shortcakes

MAKES: 4

PREP: 25 MINS

COOKING: 25 MINS

Ingredients

2 tbsp butter, cut into small pieces, plus extra for greasing

generous 1 cup all-purpose flour, plus extra for dusting

½ tsp salt

1 tsp baking powder

1 tbsp superfine sugar

¼ cup milk

confectioners' sugar, for dusting

FILLING

3 dessert apples, peeled, cored, and sliced

½ cup superfine sugar

1 tbsp lemon juice

1 tsp ground cinnamon

1¼ cups water

⅔ cup heavy cream, lightly whipped

Preheat the oven to 425°F/220°C. Lightly grease a cookie sheet. Sift the flour, salt, and baking powder into a large bowl. Stir in the sugar, then add the butter and rub it in with your fingertips until the mixture resembles fine bread crumbs. Pour in the milk and mix to a soft dough.

On a lightly floured counter, knead the dough lightly, then roll out to ½-inch/1-cm thick. Stamp out 4 circles, using a 2-inch/5-cm cutter. Transfer the circles to the prepared cookie sheet.

Bake in the oven for 15 minutes, until the shortcakes are well risen and lightly browned. Let cool.

To make the filling, place the apple, sugar, lemon juice, and cinnamon in a pan. Add the water, bring to a boil and let simmer, uncovered, for 5-10 minutes, or until the apples are tender. Cool slightly, then remove the apples from the pan.

To serve, split the shortcakes in half. Place each bottom half on an individual serving plate and spoon on a quarter of the apple slices, then the cream. Place the other half of the shortcake on top. Serve dusted with confectioners' sugar.

81

Apricot Slices

Ingredients

PIE DOUGH

⅓ cup vegan margarine, cut into small pieces, plus extra for greasing

1¾ cups whole-wheat flour

½ cup finely ground mixed nuts

4 tbsp water

soy milk, to glaze

FILLING

1 cup dried apricots

grated zest of 1 orange

1¼ cups apple juice

1 tsp ground cinnamon

⅓ cup raisins

Lightly grease a 9-inch/23-cm square cake pan. To make the pie dough, place the flour and nuts in a mixing bowl and rub in the margarine with your fingertips until the mixture resembles bread crumbs. Stir in the water and bring together to form a dough. Wrap and chill in the refrigerator for 30 minutes.

To make the filling, place the apricots, orange zest, and apple juice in a pan and bring to a boil. Simmer gently for 30 minutes until the apricots are mushy. Cool slightly, then process in a food processor or blender to a paste. Alternatively, press the mixture through a fine strainer. Stir in the cinnamon and raisins.

Divide the pie dough in half, roll out one half, and use to line the bottom of the prepared pan. Spread the apricot paste over the top and brush the edges of the pastry with water. Roll out the rest of the dough to fit over the top of the apricot paste. Press down and seal the edges.

Prick the top of the pie dough with a fork and brush with soy milk. Bake in a preheated oven, 400°F/200°C, for 20-25 minutes until the pastry is golden. Let cool slightly before cutting into 12 bars. Serve the slices either warm or cold.

Shortbread Fantails

Ingredients

4½ oz/125 g butter, softened, plus
  extra for greasing

scant ¼ cup granulated sugar

generous ⅛ cup confectioners'
  sugar

1½ cups all-purpose flour, plus
  extra for dusting

salt

2 tsp orange-flower water

superfine sugar, for sprinkling

Preheat the oven to 300°F/150°C, then lightly grease an 8-inch/20-cm shallow round cake pan. Beat the butter, granulated sugar, and confectioners' sugar together in a large bowl until light and fluffy. Sift the flour and a pinch of salt into the mixture, then add the orange-flower water. Mix together to form a soft dough.

Roll out the dough on a lightly floured counter, to an 8-inch/20-cm circle and place in the prepared pan. Prick the dough well and score into 8 triangles with a round-bladed knife.

Bake in the oven for 30-35 minutes, or until the shortbread is crisp and a pale golden color.

Sprinkle with superfine sugar, then cut along the marked lines to make the 8 fantails. Let the shortbread cool before removing the pieces from the pan. Store in an airtight container for several days.

Caramel Chocolate Shortbread

MAKES: 24

PREP: 10 MINS +
1 HR
CHILLING/
SETTING

COOKING: 30 MINS

Ingredients

4 oz/115 g butter, plus extra
  for greasing

generous 1 cup all-purpose flour

generous ¼ cup golden
  superfine sugar

7 oz/200 g semisweet chocolate,
  broken into pieces

CARAMEL

6 oz/175 g butter

generous ½ cup golden
  superfine sugar

3 tbsp corn syrup

14 oz/400 g canned condensed milk

Preheat the oven to 350°F/180°C. Grease and line the bottom of a 9-inch/23-cm shallow square cake pan. Place the butter, flour, and sugar in a food processor and process until it starts to bind together. Press into the pan and level the top. Bake in the preheated oven for 20-25 minutes, or until golden.

Meanwhile, make the caramel. Place the butter, sugar, syrup, and condensed milk in a heavy-bottom pan. Heat gently until the sugar has melted. Bring to a boil, then reduce the heat and let simmer for 6-8 minutes, stirring, until very thick. Pour over the shortbread and let chill in the refrigerator for 2 hours, or until firm.

Melt the chocolate and let cool, then spread over the caramel. Let chill in the refrigerator for 2 hours, or until set. Cut the shortbread into 12 pieces using a sharp knife and serve.

MAKES: 24

PREP: 30 MINS

COOKING: 10 MINS

Lemon Drops

Ingredients

4 oz/115 g butter or margarine,
  plus extra for greasing

1 cup superfine sugar

2 tbsp lemon juice

1 tbsp finely grated lemon rind

2 tbsp water

1½ cups all-purpose flour, sifted

1 tsp baking soda

½ tsp cream of tartar

TO DECORATE

confectioners' sugar

*candied mixed fruit, chopped finely
(optional)*

Preheat the oven to 350°F/180°C. Grease a large
cookie sheet. Beat together the butter, superfine sugar,
lemon juice, lemon rind, and water.

In a separate bowl, mix together the flour, baking soda,
and cream of tartar. Add the butter mixture and blend
together well.

Spoon the cookie dough into a pastry bag fitted with a
star-shaped tip. Pipe 24 fancy drops, about the size of
a tablespoon, on to the greased cookie sheet, allowing
room for the cookies to spread during cooking. Transfer
to the preheated oven and bake for 10 minutes, or until
the lemon drops are golden brown.

Remove from the oven, then transfer to a wire rack
and let cool completely. Dust with confectioners' sugar
and sprinkle over the candied fruit, if desired.

Lemon Jumbles

MAKES: 50

PREP: 10 MINS

COOKING: 20 MINS

Ingredients

⅓ cup butter, softened, plus extra
  for greasing

generous ½ cup superfine sugar

grated zest of 1 lemon

1 egg, lightly beaten

4 tbsp lemon juice

2½ cups all-purpose flour

1 tsp baking powder

1 tbsp milk

confectioners' sugar, for dredging

Lightly grease several cookie sheets with a little butter.

In a mixing bowl, cream together the butter, superfine sugar, and lemon zest, until pale and fluffy.

Add the beaten egg and lemon juice, a little at a time, beating well after each addition.

Strain the flour and baking powder into the creamed mixture and blend together. Add the milk, mixing to form a firm dough.

Turn the dough out onto a lightly floured counter and divide into about 50 equal-size pieces.

Roll each piece into a sausage shape with your hands and twist in the middle to make an "S" shape.

Place the cookies on the prepared cookie sheets and bake in a preheated oven, 325°F/170°C, for 15-20 minutes. Let cool completely on a wire rack. Dredge generously with confectioners' sugar before serving.

Chocolate Viennese Fingers

MAKES: 30

PREP: 20 MINS +
40 MINS
COOLING/
SETTING

COOKING: 15 MINS

Ingredients

4 oz/115 g butter, softened, plus
   extra for greasing

½ cup golden confectioners'
   sugar, sifted

generous ¾ cup all-purpose flour

1 tbsp unsweetened cocoa

3½ oz/100 g semisweet chocolate,
   melted and cooled

Preheat the oven to 350°F/180°C. Grease 2 baking sheets. Beat the butter and sugar together until light and fluffy. Sift the flour and unsweetened cocoa into the bowl and work the mixture until it is a smooth, piping consistency.

Spoon into a large pastry bag fitted with a 1-inch/2.5-cm fluted tip. Pipe 2½-inch/6-cm lengths of the mixture onto the prepared baking sheets, allowing room for expansion during cooking. Bake in the preheated oven for 15 minutes, or until firm.

Let cool on the baking sheets for 2 minutes, then transfer to a wire rack to cool completely. Dip the ends of the cookies into the melted chocolate and let set before serving.

MAKES: 30

PREP: 12 MINS

COOKING: 12 MINS

Chewy Golden Cookies

Ingredients

¾ cup butter or margarine,
*   plus extra for greasing*

scant 1½ cups soft brown sugar

1 cup corn syrup

3 egg whites

6 cups rolled oats

2 cups all-purpose flour

pinch of salt

1 tsp baking powder

confectioners' sugar, to drizzle

Preheat the oven to 350°F/180°C and grease a large cookie sheet.

In a large mixing bowl, blend the butter (or margarine, if using), sugar, syrup and egg whites together. Gradually add the oats, flour, salt, and baking powder and mix thoroughly.

Drop 30 rounded tablespoonfuls of the mixture onto the cookie sheet and transfer to the preheated oven.

Bake for 12 minutes, or until the cookies are light brown.

Remove from the oven and let them cool on a wire rack. Drizzle over the confectioners' sugar and serve.

Nutty Chocolate Drizzles

MAKES: 24

PREP: 10 MINS

COOKING: 12 MINS

Ingredients

1 cup butter or margarine,
  plus extra for greasing

1½ cups raw brown sugar

1 egg

1 cup all-purpose flour, sifted

1 tsp baking powder

1 tsp baking soda

1½ cups rolled oats

¼ cup bran

¼ cup wheatgerm

¾ cup mixed nuts, toasted
  and chopped coarsely

scant 1¼ cups semisweet
  chocolate chips

⅔ cup raisins and golden raisins

1 cup semisweet chocolate,
  chopped coarsely

Preheat the oven to 350°F/180°C. Grease a large cookie sheet. In a large bowl, cream together the butter, sugar, and egg. Add the flour, baking powder, baking soda, oats, bran, and wheatgerm and mix together until well combined. Stir in the nuts, chocoate chips, and dried fruit.

Put 24 rounded tablespoonfuls of the cookie mixture onto the greased cookie sheet. Transfer to the preheated oven and bake for 12 minutes, or until the cookies are golden brown.

Remove the cookies from the oven, then transfer to a wire rack and let them cool. While they are cooling, put the chocolate pieces into a heatproof bowl over a pan of gently simmering water and heat until melted. Stir the chocolate, then let cool slightly. Use a spoon to drizzle the chocolate in waves over the cookies, or spoon it into a piping nozzle and pipe zigzag lines over the cookies. Store in an airtight container in the refrigerator before serving.

Savory Bites

Of course the pleasures of home baking are not all about

sweet things and this chapter is brimming with tasty savory ideas for

party nibbles, lunchtime snacks, picnic treats, and after-school fillers.

Cheese is top of the list for flavorings, whether classic

Cheese Straws (see page 114) to serve with pre-dinner drinks or the less

familiar but no less delightful Cheese & Mustard Biscuits (see page 105)

for a weekend brunch table. However, don't worry if cheese is not your

favorite as there are lots of other fabulous flavors, such as spicy

Savory Curried Crackers (see page 112), aromatic Pesto Palmiers

(see page 117), and superb Bacon & Cornmeal Muffins (see page 106).

There are also recipes for timeless treats. There can be no better way to

start the morning than with Fresh Croissants (see page 96) and no better

way to end the afternoon than with Teacakes (see page 98).

Fresh Croissants

MAKES: 12

PREP: 12 HRS

COOKING: 15-20 MINS

Ingredients

1 lb 2 oz/500 g white bread flour, plus extra for rolling

scant ¼ cup superfine sugar

1 tsp salt

2 tsp active dry yeast

1¼ cups milk, heated until just warm to the touch

10½ oz/300 g butter, softened, plus extra for greasing

1 egg, lightly beaten with 1 tbsp milk, for glazing

Preheat the oven to 400°F/200°C. Stir the dry ingredients into a large bowl, make a well in the center, and add the milk. Mix to a soft dough, adding more milk if too dry. Knead on a lightly floured counter for 5-10 minutes, or until smooth and elastic. Let rise in a large greased bowl, covered, in a warm place until doubled in size. Meanwhile, flatten the butter with a rolling pin between 2 sheets of waxed paper to form a rectangle about ¼ inch/5 mm thick, then let chill.

Knead the dough for 1 minute. Remove the butter from the refrigerator and let soften slightly. Roll out the dough on a well floured counter to 18 x 6 inches/ 46 x 15 cm. Place the butter in the center, folding up the sides and squeezing the edges together gently. With the short end of the dough toward you, fold the top third down toward the center, then fold the bottom third up. Rotate 90° clockwise so that the fold is to your left and the top flap toward your right. Roll out to a rectangle and fold again. If the butter feels soft, wrap the dough in plastic wrap, and let chill. Repeat the rolling process twice more. Cut the dough in half. Roll out one half into a triangle ¼ inch/5 mm thick (keep the other half refrigerated). Use a cardboard triangular template, base 7 inches/18 cm and sides 8 inches/20 cm, to cut out the croissants.

Brush the triangles lightly with the glaze. Roll into croissant shapes, starting at the base and tucking the point underneath to prevent unrolling while cooking. Brush again with the glaze. Place on an ungreased baking sheet and let double in size. Bake for 15-20 minutes until golden brown.

SERVES: 12

PREP: 30 MINS +
3 HRS
RISING/
COOLING

COOKING: 20 MINS

Teacakes

Ingredients

*2 tbsp butter, cut into small pieces,
plus extra for greasing*

*3 cups strong white bread flour,
plus extra for dusting*

⅙-oz/7-g envelope active dry yeast

¼ cup superfine sugar

1 tsp salt

1¼ cups lukewarm milk

2¾ oz/75 g luxury dry fruit mix

honey, for brushing

butter, to serve

Grease several cookie sheets with a little butter. Sift the flour into a large bowl. Stir in the yeast, sugar, and salt. Add the butter and rub it in with your fingertips until the mixture resembles fine bread crumbs. Add the milk and mix together to form a soft dough.

Place the dough on a lightly floured counter and knead for 5 minutes. Alternatively, knead the dough with an electric mixer with a dough hook. Place the dough in a greased bowl, cover, and let rise in a warm place for 1-1½ hours, or until it has doubled in size.

Knead the dough again for a few minutes, then knead in the fruit. Divide the dough into 12 circles and place on the cookie sheets. Cover and let stand for an additional 1 hour, or until springy to the touch.

Preheat the oven to 400°F/200°C, then bake the teacakes for 20 minutes. Brush with honey while still warm, then transfer the teacakes to a wire rack to cool completely before serving them split in half and toasted, if wished. Spread with butter and serve.

Sun-dried Tomato Rolls

Ingredients

⅓ cup butter, melted and cooled slightly, plus extra for greasing

generous 1½ cups strong white bread flour, plus extra for dusting

½ tsp salt

1 envelope active dry yeast

3 tbsp lukewarm milk

2 eggs, beaten lightly

1¾ oz/50 g sun-dried tomatoes in oil, drained and finely chopped

milk, for brushing

Lightly grease a cookie sheet with a little butter.

Strain the flour and salt into a large mixing bowl. Stir in the dry yeast, then pour in the melted butter, milk, and eggs. Bring together to form a dough.

Turn the dough out onto a lightly floured counter and knead for about 5 minutes, until smooth. Alternatively, use an electric mixer with a dough hook.

Place the dough in a greased bowl, cover, and let rise in a warm place for 1-1½ hours, or until the dough has doubled in size.

Punch down the dough for 2-3 minutes. Knead the sun-dried tomatoes into the dough, sprinkling the counter with extra flour, because the tomatoes are quite oily.

Divide the dough into 8 even-size balls and place them on the prepared cookie sheet. Cover and let rise for about 30 minutes, or until the rolls have doubled in size.

Brush the rolls with milk and bake in a preheated oven, 450°F/230°C, for 10-15 minutes, or until they are golden brown.

Transfer the tomato rolls to a wire rack and let cool slightly before serving.

Cheesy Bread

Ingredients

2 tbsp butter, melted, plus extra
* for greasing*

1½ cups self-rising flour

1 tsp salt

1 tsp mustard powder

⅞ cup sharp cheese, grated

2 tbsp snipped fresh chives

1 egg, beaten

⅔ cup milk

Preheat the oven to 375°F/190°C. Grease a
9-inch/23-cm square cake pan with a little butter
and line the bottom with parchment paper.

Sift the flour, salt, and mustard powder into a large
bowl. Set aside 3 tablespoons of the grated sharp
cheese for sprinkling, then stir the remaining grated
cheese into the bowl, together with the snipped
chives. Mix together well. Add the beaten egg,
melted butter, and milk to the dry ingredients and
stir thoroughly to combine.

Pour into the prepared pan and spread with
a knife. Sprinkle over the reserved grated cheese.

Bake in the preheated oven for 30 minutes. Let the
bread cool slightly in the pan. Turn out onto a wire
rack to cool completely. Cut into triangles to serve.

SERVES: 8

PREP: 25 MINS +
30 MINS
COOLING

COOKING: 30 MINS

Cheese & Chive Biscuits

Ingredients

3 tbsp butter, plus extra
    for greasing

generous ¾ cup white self-rising
    flour, plus extra for dusting

generous ¾ cup whole-wheat
    self-rising flour

1 tsp baking powder

pinch of salt

generous ¾ cup finely grated
    Cheddar cheese

2 tbsp snipped fresh chives

3 tbsp milk

fresh chives, to garnish

Preheat the oven to 425°F/220°C, then grease a cookie sheet. Sift the 2 flours, baking powder, and salt into a bowl. Rub in the butter until the mixture resembles fine bread crumbs, then stir in the grated cheese and chives. Stir in up to 1 tablespoon of milk to make a fairly soft, light dough.

On a floured counter, roll out the dough to ¾-inch/ 2-cm thick and stamp into circles with a 2½-inch/6-cm plain cutter. Gather the trimmings, re-roll, and stamp out more biscuits until the dough is used up.

Place the biscuits on the prepared cookie sheet, brush the tops with the remaining milk, and sprinkle with the grated cheese. Bake in the preheated oven for 10 minutes, or until well risen and golden. Garnish with fresh chives and serve warm or cold.

Cheese & Mustard Biscuits

MAKES: 8
PREP: 15 MINS
COOKING: 15 MINS

Ingredients

4 tbsp butter, diced, plus extra
   for greasing

generous 1½ cups self-rising flour,
   plus extra for dusting

1 tsp baking powder

pinch of salt

1¼ cups grated sharp cheese

1 tsp mustard powder

⅔ cup milk, plus extra for brushing

pepper

Lightly grease a cookie sheet with a little butter.

Strain the flour, baking powder, and salt into a mixing bowl. Rub in the butter with your fingertips until the mixture resembles bread crumbs.

Stir in the grated cheese, mustard powder, and enough milk to form a soft dough.

Knead the dough very lightly on a lightly floured counter. Flatten it out with the palm of your hand to a depth of about 1 inch/2.5 cm.

Cut the dough into 8 wedges with a knife. Brush the wedges with a little milk and sprinkle with pepper to taste.

Bake in a preheated oven, 425°F/220°C, for 10-15 minutes, until the biscuits are golden brown.

Transfer the biscuits to a wire rack and let cool slightly before serving.

Bacon & Cornmeal Muffins

Ingredients

5½ oz/150 g pancetta

generous 1 cup self-rising flour

1 tbsp baking powder

1 tsp salt

1⅔ cups fine cornmeal

¼ cup golden granulated sugar

4 oz/115 g butter, melted

2 eggs, beaten

1¼ cups milk

Preheat the oven to 400°F/200°C and preheat the broiler to medium. Line 12 holes of 1 or 2 muffin pans with paper muffin cases. Cook the pancetta under the preheated broiler until crisp, then crumble into pieces and set aside until required.

Sift the flour, baking powder, and salt into a bowl, then stir in the cornmeal and sugar. Place the butter, eggs, and milk in a separate bowl. Add the wet ingredients to the dry ingredients and mix until just blended.

Fold in the pancetta, then divide the mixture between the paper cases and bake in the preheated oven for 20-25 minutes, or until risen and golden. Serve the muffins warm or cold.

Cheese Muffins

Ingredients

generous ¾ cup self-rising flour

1 tbsp baking powder

1 tsp salt

1½ cups fine cornmeal

1½ cups grated mature Cheddar cheese

2 oz/55 g butter, melted

2 eggs, beaten

1 garlic clove, crushed

1¼ cups milk

Preheat the oven to 400°F/200°C. Line 10 holes of 1 or 2 muffin pans with paper muffin cases. Sift the flour, baking powder, and salt into a bowl, then stir in the cornmeal and a generous 1 cup of the cheese.

Place the melted butter, eggs, crushed garlic, and milk in a separate bowl. Add the wet ingredients to the dry ingredients and mix gently until just combined.

Using a spoon, divide the mixture between the paper cases, scatter over the remaining cheese, and bake in the preheated oven for 20-25 minutes, or until risen and golden brown. Serve warm or cold.

Doughnut Muffins

MAKES: 12

PREP: 15 MINS

COOKING: 15-20 MINS

Ingredients

6 oz/175 g butter, softened, plus extra for greasing

1 cup superfine sugar

2 large eggs, lightly beaten

generous 2½ cups all-purpose flour

¾ tbsp baking powder

¼ tsp baking soda

pinch of salt

½ tsp freshly grated nutmeg

generous 1 cup milk

TOPPING

½ cup superfine sugar

1 tsp ground cinnamon

2 tbsp butter, melted

Preheat the oven to 350°F/180°C. Grease a deep 12-cup muffin pan.

In a large bowl, beat the butter and sugar together until light and creamy. Add the eggs, a little at a time, beating well between additions.

Sift the flour, baking powder, baking soda, salt, and nutmeg together. Add half to the creamed mixture with half of the milk. Gently fold the ingredients together before incorporating the remaining flour and milk. Spoon the mixture into the prepared muffin pan, filling each hole to about two-thirds full. Bake for 15-20 minutes, or until the muffins are lightly brown and firm to the touch.

For the topping, mix the sugar and cinnamon together. While the muffins are still warm from the oven, brush lightly with melted butter, and sprinkle over the cinnamon and sugar mixture. Eat warm or cold.

Savory Curried Crackers

Ingredients

⅓ cup butter, softened, plus extra
  for greasing

¾ cup all-purpose flour

1 tsp salt

2 tsp curry powder

1 cup grated mellow hard cheese

1 cup freshly grated Parmesan
  cheese

Lightly grease about 4 cookie sheets with a little butter.

Strain the all-purpose flour and salt into a mixing bowl.

Stir in the curry powder and both the grated cheeses.
Add the softened butter and rub it in with your
fingertips until the mixture comes together to form a
soft dough.

On a lightly floured counter, roll out the dough thinly to
form a rectangle.

Using a 2-inch/5-cm cookie cutter, cut out 40 crackers.

Arrange the crackers on the cookie sheets.

Bake in a preheated oven, 350°F/180°C, for
10-15 minutes.

Let the crackers cool slightly on the cookie sheets.
Transfer the crackers to a wire rack until completely
cold and crisp, then serve.

Cheese & Rosemary Sables

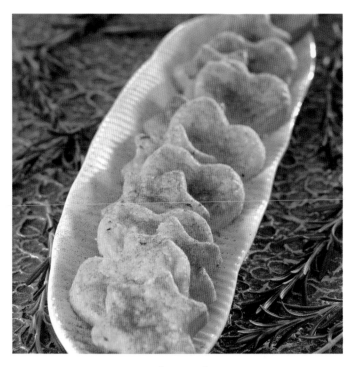

Ingredients

8 oz/225 g cold butter, diced, plus extra for greasing

1¾ cups all-purpose flour

2½ cups grated Gruyère cheese

½ tsp cayenne pepper

2 tsp finely chopped fresh rosemary leaves

1 egg yolk, beaten with 1 tbsp water

MAKES: 40

PREP: 15 MINS + 30 MINS COOLING

COOKING: 10 MINS

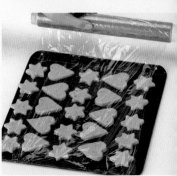

Preheat the oven to 350°F/180°C, then grease 2 cookie sheets. Place the flour, butter, cheese, cayenne pepper, and rosemary in a food processor. Pulse until the mixture forms a dough, adding a little cold water, if necessary, to bring the mixture together.

On a floured counter, roll out the dough to ¼-inch/5-mm thick. Stamp out shapes such as stars and hearts with 2½-inch/6-cm cutters.

Place the shapes on the prepared cookie sheets, then cover with plastic wrap and let chill in the refrigerator for 30 minutes, or until firm. Brush with the beaten egg yolk and bake in the oven for 10 minutes, or until golden brown. Let cool on the cookie sheets for 2 minutes, then serve warm or transfer to wire racks to cool.

Cheese Straws

Ingredients

generous ¾ cup all-purpose flour,
  plus extra for dusting

pinch of salt

1 tsp curry powder

2 oz/55 g butter, plus extra
  for greasing

½ cup grated Cheddar cheese

1 egg, beaten

poppy and cumin seeds,
  for sprinkling

Sift the flour, salt, and curry powder into a bowl. Add the butter and rub in until the mixture resembles bread crumbs. Add the cheese and half the egg and mix to form a dough. Wrap in plastic wrap and chill in the refrigerator for 30 minutes.

Preheat the oven to 400°F/200°C, then grease several cookie sheets. On a floured counter, roll out the dough to ¼-inch/5-mm thick. Cut into 3 x ½-inch/ 7.5 x 1-cm strips. Pinch the strips lightly along the sides and place on the prepared cookie sheets.

Brush the straws with the remaining egg and sprinkle half with poppy seeds and half with cumin seeds. Bake in the preheated oven for 10-15 minutes, or until golden. Transfer to wire racks to cool.

MAKES: 24

PREP: 20 MINS +
           30 MINS
           CHILLING

COOKING: 10-15 MINS

MAKES: 20

PREP: 15 MINS +
45 MINS
CHILLING
(OPTIONAL)

COOKING: 20 MINS

Spiced Cocktail Bites

Ingredients

4 oz/115 g butter, plus extra
for greasing

1 cup all-purpose flour, plus extra
for dusting

2 tsp curry powder

generous ¾ cup grated
Cheddar cheese

2 tsp poppy seeds

1 tsp black onion seeds

1 egg yolk

cumin seeds, for sprinkling

Preheat the oven to 375°F/190°C, then grease
2 cookie sheets. Sift the flour and curry powder into a
bowl. Cut the butter into pieces and add to the flour.
Rub in until the mixture resembles bread crumbs,
then stir in the cheese, poppy seeds, and black onion
seeds. Stir in the egg yolk and mix to a firm dough.

Wrap the dough in plastic wrap and chill in the
refrigerator for 30 minutes. On a floured counter, roll
out the dough to ⅛-inch/3-mm thick. Stamp out shapes
with a cutter. Re-roll the trimmings and stamp out
more cookies until the dough is used up.

Place the cookies on the prepared cookie sheets and
sprinkle with the cumin seeds. Let chill for an
additional 15 minutes. Bake in the preheated oven for
20 minutes, or until crisp and golden. Serve warm or
transfer to wire racks to cool.

Pesto Palmiers

Ingredients

butter, for greasing

all-purpose flour, for dusting

9 oz/250 g ready-made puff pastry

3 tbsp green or red pesto

*1 egg yolk, beaten with
1 tbsp water*

*¼ cup freshly grated
Parmesan cheese*

MAKES: 20

PREP: 10 MINS +
20 MINS
CHILLING

COOKING: 10 MINS

Preheat the oven to 400°F/200°C, then grease a cookie sheet. On a floured counter, roll out the pastry to a 14 x 6-inch/35 x 15-cm rectangle and trim the edges with a sharp knife. Spread the pesto evenly over the pastry. Roll up the ends tightly to meet in the center of the pastry.

Wrap in plastic wrap and chill in the refrigerator for 20 minutes, until firm, then remove from the refrigerator and unwrap. Brush with the beaten egg yolk on all sides. Cut across into ½-inch/1-cm thick slices. Place the slices on the prepared cookie sheet.

Bake in the preheated oven for 10 minutes, or until crisp and golden. Remove from the oven and immediately sprinkle over the Parmesan cheese. Serve the palmiers warm or transfer to a wire rack and let cool to room temperature.

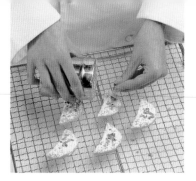

Cheese & Peanut Crescents

MAKES: 24

PREP: 10 MINS + 2 HRS CHILLING

COOKING: 15 MINS

Ingredients

3 cups all-purpose flour, plus extra for dusting

pinch of salt

1 cup peanut butter

4 cups hard cheese (e.g. Cheddar), finely grated

1¼ cups butter or margarine, plus extra for greasing

1 tsp almond extract

DECORATION

mixed nuts, toasted and chopped coarsely

confectioners' sugar

In a large bowl, sift together the flour and salt. Add the peanut butter, cheese, butter (or margarine, if using), and almond extract. Mix together until thoroughly combined, then cover with plastic wrap and refrigerate for 2 hours.

Preheat the oven to 350°F/180°C. Grease a large cookie sheet. Lightly flour a board or work surface. Cut the dough into 24 small pieces and, using your hands, roll each piece into a ball about 1 inch/2.5 cm in diameter. Then roll out each ball into a circle about ⅛ inch/3 mm in thickness. Using a knife, cut a crescent moon out of each circle by removing about one fourth of the dough from each one. Put the crescents onto the cookie sheet, then transfer to the oven and bake for 15 minutes, or until golden brown.

Remove the cookies from the oven and transfer to a wire rack, then sprinkle over the nuts and confectioners' sugar and set aside to cool.

Cheese & Apple Tart

SERVES: 8

PREP: 15 MINS

COOKING: 50 MINS

Ingredients

butter, for greasing

1½ cups self-rising flour

1 tsp baking powder

pinch of salt

⅓ cup brown sugar

generous 1 cup pitted dates, chopped

1lb 2 oz/500 g dessert apples, cored and chopped

¼ cup chopped walnuts

¼ cup sunflower oil

2 eggs

1¾ cups grated Red Leicester or Cheddar cheese

Grease a 9½-inch/23-cm loose-bottomed tart pan with a little butter and line with baking parchment.

Strain the flour, baking powder, and salt into a large bowl. Stir in the brown sugar and the chopped dates, apples, and walnuts. Mix together until thoroughly combined.

Beat the oil and eggs together and add the mixture to the dry ingredients. Stir with a wooden spoon until well combined.

Spoon half of the mixture into the prepared pan and level the surface with the back of a spoon.

Sprinkle with the grated cheese, then spoon over the remaining cake mix, spreading it to the edges of the pan.

Bake in a preheated oven, 350°F/180°C, for 45-50 minutes or until golden and firm to the touch.

Let the tart cool slightly in the pan. Remove the tart from the pan and serve warm.

Festive Feasts

Birthdays, anniversaries, graduation day, or Christmas, we all love to

celebrate with something special to eat and, more often than not, the

centerpiece is a truly splendid cake. Festivals and family occasions provide

a wonderful opportunity to show off your home baking skills and this

chapter offers plenty of scope. For example, if you don't have the time or

the confidence to tackle a traditional iced Christmas Cake (see page 124),

why not make a charming but less demanding Yule Log (see page 130)?

Choose from a global array of cakes and desserts – Viennese Sachertorte

(see page 126), Australian Mixed Fruit Pavlova (see page 139), or

Italian Cherry & Chocolate Tiramisu (see page 140).

Don't overlook other traditional baked goodies, whether Hot Cross Buns

(see page 164) and Easter Cookies (see page 156) for Holy Week,

Festive Mince Pies (see page 150) and Lebkuchen (see page 162) for

Christmas, or Party Cookies (see page 158) for any time of year.

Christmas Cake

Ingredients

scant 1 cup raisins

generous ⅔ cup pitted dates, chopped

generous ⅔ cup golden raisins

½ cup candied cherries, rinsed

⅔ cup brandy

1 cup butter, plus extra for greasing

1 cup superfine sugar

4 eggs

grated zest of 1 orange and 1 lemon

1 tbsp molasses

generous 1½ cups all-purpose flour

½ tsp salt

½ tsp baking powder

1 tsp allspice

scant ¼ cup toasted almonds, chopped

scant ¼ cup toasted hazelnuts, chopped

4½ cups confectioners' sugar

1 egg white

juice of 1 lemon

1 tsp vanilla extract

holly leaves, to decorate

MAKES: 1 (8-INCH/ 20-CM CAKE)

PREP: 45 MINS + 8 HRS SOAKING

COOKING: 3 HRS

Make this cake at least 3 weeks in advance. Put all the fruit in a bowl, pour over the brandy, and soak overnight.

Preheat the oven to 225°F/110°C. Grease an 8-inch/20-cm cake pan and line it with waxed paper. In a bowl, cream together the butter and sugar until fluffy. Gradually beat in the eggs. Stir in the citrus zest and molasses. In a separate bowl, sift together the flour, salt, baking powder, and allspice, then fold into the egg mixture. Fold in the fruit, brandy, and nuts, then spoon into the cake pan. Bake for at least 3 hours. If it browns too quickly, cover with foil. The cake is cooked when a skewer inserted into the center comes out clean. Remove from the oven and cool on a wire rack. Store in an airtight container until required.

To make the icing, put the sugar, egg white, lemon juice, and vanilla into a bowl and mix until smooth. Spread over the cake, using a fork to give texture. Decorate with holly leaves.

Sachertorte

Ingredients

4 oz/115 g unsalted butter,
  softened, plus extra for greasing

6 oz/175 g semisweet chocolate,
  broken into pieces

3 tbsp black coffee

¾ cup golden superfine sugar

5 eggs, separated

1 cup all-purpose flour, sifted

4 tbsp apricot jelly

dash of lemon juice

1 tbsp water

FROSTING

⅜ cup golden superfine sugar

4 tbsp water

3½ oz/100 g semisweet chocolate,
  broken into pieces

Preheat the oven to 325°F/160°C. Grease and line a 9-inch/23-cm round cake pan. Heat the chocolate in a pan with the coffee until melted, stir, and cool. Beat the butter and ⅜ cup of the sugar in a bowl until fluffy. Beat in the chocolate mixture and egg yolks. Stir in the flour. Whisk the egg whites in a separate bowl until stiff. Whisk in the remaining sugar. Fold into the cake batter. Turn into the pan and bake for 1–1¼ hours, until firm. Let stand in the pan for 5 minutes. Turn out onto a wire rack to cool.

Slice the cake in half horizontally. Sandwich together with half the jelly. Heat the remaining jelly, lemon juice, and water in a pan until the jelly has melted. Strain into a bowl then brush over the top and sides of the cake.

For the frosting, heat the sugar and water until boiling and stir until the sugar has dissolved. Remove from the heat, add the chocolate, and stir until smooth. Return to the heat and boil to a temperature of 241°F/116°C on a sugar thermometer. Remove from the heat, stir until the mixture stops bubbling, then pour all but 2 tablespoons quickly over the top of the cake, letting it flow down the sides. Smooth round the sides, but do not touch the top. When the frosting starts to set, warm the reserved frosting and drip "Sacher" over the top from the tip of a knife.

SERVES:	8-10
PREP:	25 MINS + 2 HRS SETTING
COOKING:	1 HR 10 MINS- 1 HR 25 MINS

Panforte Di Siena

SERVES: *12-16*

PREP: *10 MINS +*
20 MINS
COOLING

COOKING: *35-40 MINS*

Ingredients

butter, for greasing

¼ cup candied cherries, quartered

*⅔ cup mixed candied orange and
lemon peel, finely chopped*

*2 tbsp candied ginger,
coarsely chopped*

1 cup slivered almonds

*¾ cup hazelnuts, toasted
and coarsely ground*

⅜ cup all-purpose flour

¼ cup unsweetened cocoa

1 tsp ground cinnamon

¼ tsp ground cloves

¼ tsp ground nutmeg

¼ tsp ground coriander

⅓ cup honey

*generous ½ cup golden
superfine sugar*

1 tsp orange flower water

confectioners' sugar, for dusting

Preheat the oven to 325°F/160°C. Thoroughly grease the bottom of an 8-inch/20-cm loose-bottom cake or tart pan. Line the bottom with nonstick parchment paper. Place the cherries, candied peel, ginger, almonds, and hazelnuts in a bowl. Sift in the flour, cocoa, cinnamon, cloves, nutmeg, and coriander, and mix. Set aside.

Place the honey, sugar, and orange flower water in a pan and heat gently until the sugar has dissolved. Bring the mixture to a boil and boil steadily until a temperature of 241°F/116°C has been reached on a sugar thermometer, or a small amount of the mixture forms a soft ball when dropped into cold water.

Quickly remove the pan from the heat and stir in the dry ingredients. Mix thoroughly and turn into the prepared pan. Spread evenly and bake in the preheated oven for 30 minutes. Let cool in the pan. Turn out and carefully peel away the lining paper. Dust confectioners' sugar lightly over the top and cut into wedges to serve.

Yule Log

Ingredients

butter, for greasing

3 eggs

generous ½ cup golden superfine sugar

generous ⅓ cup all-purpose flour

¼ cup unsweetened cocoa, plus extra to dust

Chocolate Caraque

2 oz/55 g white chocolate, melted

confectioners' sugar, for dusting

SYRUP

generous ¼ cup golden superfine sugar

⅔ cup water

4 tbsp Cointreau

FROSTING

2 oz/55 g butter, softened

generous 1 cup confectioners' sugar, sifted

grated rind of 1 orange

1 tbsp Cointreau

BUTTERCREAM

1 tbsp unsweetened cocoa

1 tbsp boiling water

3 oz/85 g butter

1½ cups confectioners' sugar, sifted

Preheat the oven to 400°F/200°C. Grease and line an 8 x 12-inch/20 x 30-cm jelly roll pan. Whisk the eggs and sugar together until thick and a trail is left when the whisk is lifted. Sift the flour and unsweetened cocoa together into a separate bowl, then fold into the egg mixture. Turn into the pan and bake for 8-10 minutes, or until the cake springs back when lightly pressed. Roll up the sponge and let cool.

To make the syrup, heat the sugar and water in a pan until the sugar dissolves. Boil for 2 minutes. Stir in the Cointreau and let cool. Unroll the sponge and remove the paper. Sprinkle the sponge with syrup. To make the frosting, beat the butter until creamy. Beat in the other ingredients until smooth. Spread over the sponge and roll up.

To make the buttercream, place the cocoa in a heatproof bowl and stir in the water. Let cool. Beat the butter in a separate bowl until creamy. Gradually beat in the confectioners' sugar and cocoa until smooth. Cut off a quarter of the roll diagonally and attach to the side of the roll with buttercream. Cover the roll with buttercream and mark lines to represent bark. Cover with Chocolate Caraque (see below). Pipe white chocolate spirals on to the ends. Dust with cocoa and confectioners' sugar and serve.

To make the Chocolate Caraque spread a thin layer of melted chocolate onto a flat surface and just then it appears to have set, but is in fact still soft, hold a knife at a 45° angle to the surface and push it along to form scrolls.

SERVES: 8

PREP: 35 MINS + 30 MINS COOLING

COOKING: 16-18 MINS

Cup Cakes

Ingredients

generous ¾ cup water

3 oz/85 g butter

⅜ cup golden superfine sugar

1 tbsp corn syrup

3 tbsp milk

1 tsp vanilla extract

1 tsp baking soda

2 tbsp unsweetened cocoa

generous 1½ cups all-purpose flour

FROSTING

1¾ oz/50 g semisweet chocolate,
  broken into pieces

4 tbsp water

1¾ oz/50 g butter

1¾ oz/50 g white chocolate,
  broken into pieces

3 cups confectioners' sugar

TO DECORATE

candied rose petals

candied violets

Preheat the oven to 350°F/180°C. Place paper cake cases in 2 muffin pans. Place the water, butter, sugar, and syrup in a pan. Heat gently, stirring, until the sugar has dissolved, then bring to a boil. Reduce the heat and cook gently for 5 minutes. Remove from the heat and let cool. Place the milk and vanilla extract in a bowl. Add the baking soda and stir to dissolve. Sift the unsweetened cocoa and flour into a separate bowl and add the syrup mixture. Stir in the milk and beat until smooth.

Carefully spoon the batter into the paper cases to within two-thirds of the tops. Bake in the oven for 20 minutes, or until well risen and firm to the touch. Let cool on a wire rack. To make the frosting, place the semisweet chocolate in a small heatproof bowl with half the water and half the butter and set the bowl over a pan of gently simmering water until melted. Stir until smooth and let stand over the water. Repeat with the white chocolate and remaining water and butter.

Stir half the confectioners' sugar into each bowl and beat until smooth and fudgy. Divide the frostings between the cakes, filling to the top of the paper cases. Let cool, then place a rose petal on each of the semisweet chocolate frosted cakes and a violet on each white chocolate frosted cake. Let set before serving.

Giggle Cake

SERVES: 8

PREP: 25 MINS

COOKING: 1 HR 15 MINS

Ingredients

12 oz/350g mixed dried fruit

generous ½ cup butter or margarine, plus extra for greasing

¾ cup brown sugar

2 cups self-rising flour

pinch of salt

2 eggs, beaten

8 oz/225 g can chopped pineapple, drained

¾ cup candied cherries, halved

Put the mixed dried fruit into a large bowl and cover with boiling water. Set aside to soak for 10-15 minutes, then drain well.

Put the butter or margarine and sugar into a large pan and heat gently until melted. Add the drained mixed dried fruit and cook over low heat, stirring frequently, for 4-5 minutes. Remove from the heat and transfer to a mixing bowl. Set aside to cool.

Sift together the flour and salt into the dried fruit mixture and stir well. Add the eggs, mixing until the ingredients are thoroughly incorporated.

Add the pineapples and cherries to the cake mixture and stir to combine. Transfer to a greased and lined 2 lb/1 kg loaf pan and level the surface.

Bake in a preheated oven, 350°F/180°C, for about 1 hour. Test the cake with a fine toothpick; if it comes out clean, the cake is cooked. If not, return to the oven for a few more minutes. Transfer the cake to a wire rack to cool completely before serving.

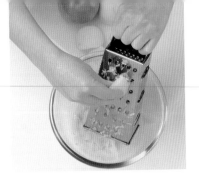

Spiced Apple Tart

SERVES: 4

PREP: 20 MINS +
30 MINS
RESTING

COOKING: 35 MINS

Ingredients

PIE DOUGH

scant 1½ cups all-purpose flour, plus extra for dusting

scant ½ cup butter, diced, plus extra for greasing

scant ½ cup confectioner's sugar, sifted

finely grated zest of 1 lemon

1 egg yolk, beaten

3 tbsp milk

FILLING

3 medium tart cooking apples

2 tbsp lemon juice

finely grated zest of 1 lemon

⅔ cup honey

3 cups fresh white or whole-wheat breadcrumbs

1 tsp ground allspice

pinch of ground nutmeg

whipped cream, to serve

To make the pie dough, sift the flour into a bowl. Rub in the butter. Mix in the confectioner's sugar, lemon zest, egg yolk, and milk. Knead briefly on a lightly floured counter. Let rest for 30 minutes.

Preheat the oven to 400°F/200°C. Grease an 8-inch/20-cm tart pan with butter. Roll out the dough to a thickness of ¼ inch/5 mm and use to line the bottom and sides of the tart pan.

To make the filling, core 2 apples and grate them into a bowl. Add 1 tablespoon of lemon juice and all the lemon zest, along with the honey, breadcrumbs, and allspice. Mix together well. Spoon evenly into the tart shell. Core and slice the remaining apple, and use to decorate the top of the tart. Brush the apple slices with lemon juice, then sprinkle over the nutmeg. Bake in the preheated oven for 35 minutes, or until firm. Remove from the oven and serve with whipped cream.

Dark & White Chocolate Torte

SERVES: 6

PREP: 20 MINS +
1 HR 20 MINS
COOLING/
SETTING

COOKING: 35-40 MINS

Ingredients

4 eggs

½ cup superfine sugar

¾ cup all-purpose flour

FILLING

1¼ cups heavy cream

*5½ oz/150 g semisweet chocolate,
  broken into small pieces*

TOPPING

2¾ oz/75 g white chocolate

1 tbsp butter

1 tbsp milk

4 tbsp confectioners' sugar

Preheat the oven to 350°F/180°C. Grease and line the bottom of an 8-inch/20-cm round springform cake pan. Whisk the eggs and superfine sugar in a large bowl with an electric whisk for 10 minutes, or until the mixture is very light and foamy and the whisk leaves a trail that lasts a few seconds when lifted.

Sift the flour and fold in with a metal spoon or spatula. Pour into the prepared pan and bake in the oven for 35-40 minutes, or until springy to the touch. Let cool slightly, then transfer to a wire rack to cool completely.

For the filling, place the cream in a pan and bring to a boil, stirring. Add the chocolate and stir until melted. Remove from the heat, transfer to a bowl, and let cool. Beat with a wooden spoon until thick.

Slice the cold cake horizontally into 2 layers. Sandwich the layers together with the semisweet chocolate cream and place on a wire rack.

For the topping, melt the chocolate and butter together and stir until blended. Whisk in the milk and confectioners' sugar. Continue whisking for a few minutes until the frosting is cool. Pour it over the cake and spread with a spatula to coat the top and sides. Let set.

137

Raspberry Vacherin

Ingredients

3 egg whites

¾ cup superfine sugar

1 tsp cornstarch

1 oz/25 g semisweet chocolate, grated

FILLING

6 oz/175 g semisweet chocolate

2 cups heavy cream, whipped

2 cups fresh raspberries

a little melted chocolate, to decorate

Preheat the oven to 275°F/140°C. Draw 3 rectangles, 4 x 10 inches/10 x 25 cm, on sheets of parchment paper, and place on 2 cookie sheets.

Whisk the egg whites in a mixing bowl until soft peaks form, then gradually whisk in half of the sugar and continue whisking until the mixture is very stiff and glossy. Carefully fold in the rest of the sugar, the cornstarch, and the grated chocolate with a metal spoon or a spatula.

Spoon the meringue mixture into a pastry bag fitted with a ½-inch/1-cm plain tip and pipe lines across the rectangles.

Bake in the preheated oven for 1½ hours, changing the position of the cookie sheets halfway through. Without opening the oven door, turn off the oven and let the meringues cool inside the oven, then peel away the parchment paper.

To make the filling, melt the chocolate and spread it over 2 of the meringue layers. Let the filling harden.

Place 1 chocolate-coated meringue on a plate and top with about one-third of the cream and raspberries. Gently place the second chocolate-coated meringue on top and spread with half of the remaining cream and raspberries. Place the last meringue on the top and decorate with the remaining cream and raspberries. Put a few pieces of semisweet chocolate in a heatproof bowl set over a pan of gently simmering water until melted. Drizzle a little melted chocolate over the top of the vacherin and serve.

Mixed Fruit Pavlova

SERVES: 4

PREP: 30 MINS +
30 MINS
COOLING

COOKING: 3 HRS

Ingredients

6 egg whites

pinch of cream of tartar

pinch of salt

1½ cups superfine sugar

scant 2½ cups heavy cream

1 tsp vanilla extract

2 kiwifruits, peeled and sliced

9 oz/250 g strawberries, hulled and sliced

3 ripe peaches, sliced

1 ripe mango, peeled and sliced

2 tbsp orange liqueur, such as Cointreau

fresh mint leaves, to decorate

Preheat the oven to 225°F/110°C. Line 3 cookie sheets with baking parchment, then draw an 8½-inch/22-cm circle in the center of each one. Beat the egg whites into stiff peaks. Mix in the cream of tartar and salt. Gradually add 1 cup of sugar. Beat for 2 minutes until glossy. Fill a pastry bag with the mixture and use it to fill each circle, making them slightly domed in the center. Bake for 3 hours. Remove from the oven and let cool.

Whip together the cream and vanilla extract with all but 2 tablespoons of the remaining sugar. Put the fruit into a separate bowl and stir in the liqueur. Put one meringue circle onto a serving plate, then spread over one-third of the sugared cream. Spread over one-third of the fruit, then top with a meringue. Spread over another third of cream, then another third of fruit. Top with the last meringue. Spread over the remaining cream, followed by the remaining fruit. Decorate with mint leaves and serve.

SERVES:	4
PREP:	20 MINS + 2 HRS CHILLING
COOKING:	NONE

Chocolate **& Cherry Tiramisù**

Ingredients

generous ¾ cup strong black coffee, cooled to room temperature

6 tbsp cherry brandy

16 trifle sponges

1¼ mascarpone

1¼ cups heavy cream, lightly whipped

3 tbsp confectioner's sugar

9½ oz/275 g sweet cherries, halved and pitted

2¼ oz/60 g chocolate, curls or grated

whole cherries, to decorate

Pour the cooled coffee into a pitcher and stir in the cherry brandy. Put half of the trifle sponges into the bottom of a serving dish, then pour over half of the coffee mixture.

Put the mascarpone into a separate bowl along with the cream and sugar, and mix together well. Spread half of the mascarpone mixture over the coffee-soaked trifle sponges, then top with half of the cherries. Arrange the remaining trifle sponges on top. Pour over the remaining coffee mixture and top with the remaining cherries. Finish with a layer of mascarpone mixture. Scatter over the grated chocolate, cover with plastic wrap, and chill in the refrigerator for at least 2 hours.

Remove from the refrigerator, decorate with cherries, and serve.

Profiteroles

SERVES: 4

PREP: 25 MINS

COOKING: 55 MINS

Ingredients

CHOUX PASTRY

5 tbsp butter, plus extra for
  greasing

generous ¾ cup water

¾ cup all-purpose flour

3 eggs, beaten

CREAM FILLING

1¼ cups heavy cream

3 tbsp superfine sugar

1 tsp vanilla extract

CHOCOLATE & BRANDY SAUCE

4½ oz/125 g semisweet chocolate,
  broken into small pieces

2½ tbsp butter

6 tbsp water

2 tbsp brandy

Preheat the oven to 400°F/200°C. Grease a large cookie sheet with butter. To make the pastry, put the water and butter into a pan and bring to a boil. Meanwhile, sift the flour into a bowl. Remove the pan from the heat and beat in the flour until smooth. Cool for 5 minutes. Beat in enough of the eggs to give the mixture a soft, dropping consistency. Transfer into a pastry bag fitted with a ½-inch/1-cm plain tip. Pipe small balls onto the cookie sheet. Bake for 25 minutes. Remove from the oven. Pierce each ball with a skewer to let steam escape.

To make the filling, whip together the cream, sugar, and vanilla extract. Cut the pastry balls almost in half, then fill with cream.

To make the sauce, gently melt the chocolate, butter, and water together in a small pan, stirring, until smooth. Stir in the brandy. Pile the profiteroles into individual serving dishes or into a pyramid on a raised cake stand. Pour over the sauce and serve.

Strawberry Chocolate Gâteau

SERVES: 8

PREP: 25 MINS + 30 MIN COOLING

COOKING: 30-40 MINS

Ingredients

butter, for greasing

SPONGE

3 eggs

generous ½ cup golden superfine sugar

⅔ cup self-rising flour

2 tbsp unsweetened cocoa

FILLING AND TOPPING

generous 1 cup strawberries

1¼ cups heavy cream

½ tsp vanilla extract

1 tbsp confectioners' sugar

2 tbsp Kirsch

Chocolate Curls

Preheat the oven to 375°F/190°C. Grease and line an 8½-inch/22-cm cake pan. To make the sponge, place the eggs and sugar in a bowl and whisk until thick and mousse-like, and a trail is left when the whisk is lifted. Sift the flour and unsweetened cocoa into a separate bowl, then fold into the whisked cake batter. Turn into the pan and bake in the oven for 30-40 minutes, or until the cake springs back when pressed in the center. Let stand the pan for 5 minutes, then let cool on a wire rack.

Meanwhile, prepare the filling. Set aside 4 strawberries, and hull and slice the remainder. Whip the cream, vanilla extract, and confectioners' sugar together until thick. Set aside two-thirds of the cream and fold the strawberries into the remainder.

Slice the sponge horizontally into 2 layers and sprinkle each layer with 1 tablespoon of Kirsch. Place one layer on a plate and spread over the strawberry cream. Place the other sponge layer on top. Place some of the reserved cream in a pastry bag fitted with a fluted tip and spread the remainder over the top and sides of the cake. Coat the sides with Chocolate Curls. Pipe the cream round the top of the cake. Cut the reserved strawberries in half, keeping the stalks intact, and arrange on the piped cream.

Baked Chocolate Alaska

SERVES: 4

PREP: 50 MINS

COOKING: 12 MINS

Ingredients

butter, for greasing

2 eggs

4 tbsp superfine sugar

5 tbsp all-purpose flour

2 tbsp unsweetened cocoa

3 egg whites

generous ¾ cup superfine sugar

*4 cups good-quality
    chocolate ice cream*

Preheat the oven to 425°F/220°C. Grease a
7-inch/18-cm round cake pan with butter and line the
bottom with parchment paper.

Whisk the eggs and the 4 tablespoons of sugar in a
bowl until very thick and pale. Sift the flour and
cocoa together and fold in.

Pour into the prepared pan and bake in the preheated
oven for 7 minutes, or until springy to the touch.
Transfer to a wire rack to cool.

Whisk the egg whites in a spotlessly clean, greasefree
bowl until soft peaks form. Gradually add the sugar,
whisking, until you have a thick, glossy meringue.

Place the sponge on a large baking sheet and pile the
ice cream in the center in a heaped dome.

Pipe or spread the meringue over the ice cream,
making sure that the ice cream is completely
enclosed. (At this point the dessert can be frozen,
if you like.)

Return to the oven for 5 minutes, or until the
meringue is just golden. Serve immediately.

Mincemeat & Grape Jalousie

SERVES: 4

PREP: 1 HR 15 MINS

COOKING: 45 MINS

Ingredients

1 tbsp butter, for greasing

*1lb 2 oz/500 g ready-made puff
pastry dough, thawed if frozen*

14½ oz/410 g jar sweet mincemeat

*1 cup grapes, seeded and
cut in half*

1 egg, beaten lightly

raw brown sugar, for sprinkling

Lightly grease a cookie sheet with the butter.

Roll out the puff pie dough on a lightly floured counter and cut into 2 rectangles.

Place one dough rectangle on the prepared cookie sheet and brush the edges with water.

Combine the mincemeat and grapes in a mixing bowl. Spread the mixture evenly over the dough rectangle on the cookie sheet, leaving a 1-inch/2.5-cm border.

Fold the second pie dough rectangle in half lengthwise, and cut a series of parallel lines across the folded edge with a sharp knife, leaving a 1-inch/2.5-cm border.

Open out the second rectangle and lay it over the mincemeat filling. Press the edges of the pie dough together to seal.

Flute and crimp the edges of the dough with your fingers. Lightly brush with the beaten egg to glaze and sprinkle with raw brown sugar.

Bake in a preheated oven, 425°F/220°C, for 15 minutes. Reduce the heat to 350°F/180°C and cook for 30 minutes more, until the jalousie is well risen and golden brown.

Transfer to a wire rack to cool completely before serving.

Festive Mince Pies

MAKES: 12

PREP: 20 MINS

COOKING: 15 MINS

Ingredients

scant 1½ cups all-purpose flour, plus extra for dusting

scant ½ cup butter

¼ cup confectioner's sugar

1 egg yolk

2-3 tbsp milk

10½ oz/300 g mincemeat

1 egg, beaten, for sealing and glazing

confectioners' sugar, for dusting

sprigs of holly, to decorate

Preheat the oven to 350°F/180°C. Sift the flour into a mixing bowl. Using your fingertips, rub in the butter until the mixture resembles bread crumbs. Mix in the sugar and egg yolk. Stir in enough milk to make a soft dough, turn out onto a lightly floured counter, and knead lightly until smooth.

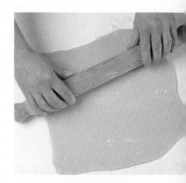

Shape the dough into a ball and roll out to a thickness of ½ inch/1 cm. Use fluted cutters to cut out 12 circles of 2¾ inches/7 cm diameter and 12 circles of 2 inches/5 cm diameter. Dust 12 tartlet pans with flour and line with the larger dough circles. Prick the bottoms with a fork, then half-fill each pie with mincemeat. Brush beaten egg around the rims, then press the smaller dough circles on top to seal. Make a small hole in the top of each one. Decorate the pies with Christmas trees made from dough trimmings. Brush all over with beaten egg, then bake for 15 minutes. Remove from the oven and cool on a wire rack. Dust with confectioners' sugar and serve.

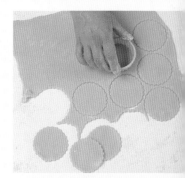

Double Chocolate Chip Cookies

MAKES: 24

PREP: 15 MINS +
20 MINS
COOLING

COOKING: 10-15 MINS

Ingredients

4 oz/115 g butter, softened,
  plus extra for greasing

¼ cup golden superfine sugar

¼ cup brown sugar

1 egg, beaten

½ tsp vanilla extract

generous ¾ cup all-purpose flour

2 tbsp unsweetened cocoa

½ tsp baking soda

⅔ cup milk chocolate chips

⅓ cup coarsely chopped walnuts

Preheat the oven to 350°F/180°C, then grease
3 cookie sheets. Place the butter, granulated sugar,
and brown sugar in a bowl and beat until light and
fluffy. Gradually beat in the egg and vanilla extract.

Sift the flour, cocoa, and baking soda into the mixture
and stir in carefully. Stir in the chocolate chips and
walnuts. Drop spoonfuls of the dough onto the
prepared cookie sheets, spaced well apart to allow
for spreading.

Bake in the oven for 10-15 minutes, or until the
mixture has spread and the cookies are starting to
feel firm. Let cool on the cookie sheets for 2 minutes,
then transfer to wire racks to cool completely.

MAKES:	36
PREP:	15 MINS + 1 HR CHILLING
COOKING:	12 MINS

Traditional Spiced Cookies

Ingredients

1½ cups all-purpose flour

2 tsp allspice

1 tsp salt

1 tsp baking soda

¾ cup butter or margarine, plus
   extra for greasing

½ cup granulated sugar

1 cup soft brown sugar, plus
   extra for dusting

2 eggs

4 tbsp milk

3½ cups rolled oats

½ cup raisins

scant ½ cup golden raisins

Mix the flour, allspice, salt, and baking soda together and sift into a large mixing bowl.

One at a time, mix in the butter (or margarine, if using), both sugars, the eggs, and the milk. Beat the mixture until it is smooth.

Add the oats and dried fruit and stir thoroughly. Cover the bowl with plastic wrap and place it in the refrigerator to chill for 1 hour.

Preheat the oven to 375°F/190°C and grease a large cookie sheet.

Put 36 tablespoonfuls of cookie mixture onto the greased cookie sheet, making sure they are well spaced. Dust lightly with soft brown sugar. Transfer to the preheated oven and bake for 12 minutes, or until the cookies are golden brown.

Remove the cookies from the oven and place on a wire rack to cool thoroughly.

Mincemeat Crumble Bars

MAKES: 12

PREP: 20 MINS + 1 HR CHILLING/ COOLING

COOKING: 32-35 MINS

Ingredients

1⅓ cups ready-made mincemeat
confectioners' sugar, for dusting

BOTTOM LAYER

5 oz/140 g butter, plus extra
   for greasing
scant ½ cup golden superfine sugar
1 cup all-purpose flour
scant ⅔ cup cornstarch

TOPPING

generous ¾ cup self-rising flour
6 tbsp butter, cut into pieces
scant ½ cup golden superfine sugar
¼ cup slivered almonds

Grease a shallow 11 x 8-inch/28 x 20-cm cake pan. To make the bottom layer, place the butter and sugar in a bowl and cream together until light and fluffy. Sift in the flour and cornstarch and, with your hands, bring the mixture together to form a ball. Push the dough into the cake pan, pressing it out and into the corners, then chill in the refrigerator for 20 minutes. Preheat the oven to 400°F/200°C. Bake the bottom layer in the oven for 12-15 minutes, or until puffed and golden.

To make the crumble topping, place the flour, butter, and sugar in a bowl and rub together into coarse crumbs. Stir in the almonds.

Spread the mincemeat over the bottom layer and scatter the crumbs on top. Bake in the oven for an additional 20 minutes, or until golden. Let cool slightly, then cut into 12 pieces and let cool completely. Dust with sifted confectioners' sugar, then serve.

Easter Cookies

Ingredients

6 oz/175 g butter, softened, plus
  extra for greasing

generous ¾ cup golden
  superfine sugar

1 egg, beaten

2 tbsp milk

¼ cup chopped candied peel

generous 2/3 cup currants

2½ cups all-purpose flour,
  plus extra for dusting

1 tsp allspice

GLAZE

1 egg white, lightly beaten

2 tbsp golden superfine sugar

Preheat the oven to 350°F/180°C, then grease
2 large cookie sheets. Place the butter and sugar in a
bowl and beat until light and fluffy. Gradually beat in
the egg and milk. Stir in the candied peel and currants,
then sift in the flour and allspice. Mix together to
make a firm dough. Knead lightly until smooth.

On a floured counter, roll out the dough to ¼-inch/
5-mm thick and use a 2-inch/5-cm round cookie
cutter to stamp out the cookies. Re-roll the dough
trimmings and stamp out more cookies until the
dough is used up. Place the cookies on the prepared
cookie sheets and bake in the preheated oven for
10 minutes.

Remove from the oven to glaze. Brush with the egg
white and sprinkle with the superfine sugar, then
return to the oven for an additional 5 minutes, or
until lightly browned. Let cool on the cookie sheets
for 2 minutes, then transfer to wire racks to cool
completely.

MAKES: 24

PREP: 20 MINS +
           20 MINS
           COOLING

COOKING: 10-15 MINS

Party Cookies

Ingredients

4 oz/115 g butter, softened, plus
  extra for greasing

generous ½ cup brown sugar

1 tbsp corn syrup

½ tsp vanilla extract

1¼ cups self-rising flour

3 oz/85 g sugar-coated
  chocolate beans

Preheat the oven to 350°F/180°C, then grease 2 cookie sheets. Place the butter and sugar in a bowl and beat together with an electric whisk until light and fluffy, then beat in the syrup and vanilla extract.

Sift in half the flour and work it into the mixture. Stir in the chocolate beans and the remaining flour and work the dough together using a spatular.

Roll the dough into 16 balls and place them on the prepared cookie sheets, spaced well apart to allow for spreading. Do not flatten them. Bake in the preheated oven for 10-12 minutes, or until pale golden at the edges. Remove from the oven and let cool on the cookie sheets for 2 minutes, then transfer to wire racks to cool completely.

Christmas Shortbread

Ingredients

½ cup superfine sugar

1cup butter, plus extra for greasing

3 cups all purpose flour, sifted, plus
  extra for dusting

pinch of salt

TO DECORATE

½ cup confectioners' sugar

silver balls

candied cherries

angelica

Beat the sugar and butter together in a large bowl until combined (thorough creaming is not necessary).

Sift in the flour and salt and work together to form a stiff dough. Turn out on to a lightly floured work surface. Knead lightly for a few moments until smooth, but avoid over-handling. Chill in the refrigerator for 10-15 minutes. Preheat the oven to180°C/350°F/ Gas Mark 4. Grease several cookie sheets.

Roll out the dough on a lightly floured work surface and cut into shapes with small Christmas cutters, such as trees, bells, stars and angels. Place on greased cookie sheets.

Bake in the oven for 10-15 minutes, until pale golden brown. Leave to cool on the cookie sheets for 10 minutes, then transfer to wire racks to cool completely.

Mix the confectioners' sugar with a little water to make a frosting, and use to frost the cookies. Before the icing sets, decorate with silver balls, tiny pieces of candied cherries and angelica. Store in an airtight container or wrap the cookies individually in cellophane, tie with colored ribbon or string, then hang them on the Christmas tree as edible decorations.

Lebkuchen

Ingredients

3 eggs

1 cup golden superfine sugar

½ cup all-purpose flour

2 tsp unsweetened cocoa

1 tsp ground cinnamon

½ tsp ground cardamom

¼ tsp ground cloves

¼ tsp ground nutmeg

generous 1 cup ground almonds

scant ⅓ cup candied peel,
  chopped finely

TO DECORATE

4 oz/115 g semisweet chocolate

4 oz/115 g white chocolate

sugar crystals

Preheat the oven to 350°F/180°C. Line several cookie sheets with nonstick parchment paper. Put the eggs and sugar in a heatproof bowl set over a pan of gently simmering water. Whisk until thick and foamy. Remove the bowl from the pan and continue to whisk for 2 minutes.

Sift the flour, cocoa, cinnamon, cardamom, cloves, and nutmeg into the bowl and stir in with the ground almonds and chopped peel. Drop heaping teaspoonfuls of the cookie dough on to the prepared cookie sheets, spreading them gently into smooth mounds.

Bake in the oven for 15-20 minutes, until light brown and slightly soft to the touch. Cool on the cookie sheets for 10 minutes, then transfer to wire racks to cool completely. Put the semisweet and white chocolate in 2 separate heatproof bowls set over 2 saucepans of gently simmering water until melted. Dip half the cookies in melted semisweet chocolate and half in white. Sprinkle with sugar crystals and let set.

Yuletide Cookies

MAKES: 24

PREP: 20 MINS + 4 HRS CHILLING

COOKING: 10 MINS

Ingredients

7 cups all-purpose flour, plus extra for dusting

1 tbsp baking soda

1 tbsp powdered ginger

3 tsp allspice

pinch of salt

1 cup butter or margarine, plus extra for greasing

1½ cups corn syrup

1 cup raw brown sugar

½ cup water

1 egg

1 tsp brandy

1 tsp very finely grated orange zest

confectioners' sugar, to decorate

In a large bowl, sift together the flour, baking soda, ginger, allspice, and salt. In a separate bowl, beat together the butter (or margarine, if using), corn syrup, sugar, water, egg, and brandy until thoroughly combined. Gradually stir in the grated orange zest, then the flour mixture.

Halve the dough, then wrap in plastic wrap and refrigerate for at least 4 hours (it will keep for up to 6 days). When ready to use, preheat the oven to 350°F/180°C and grease a cookie sheet.

Flour a board or counter. Roll each half of dough into a ball, then roll it to a thickness of ⅛ inch/3 mm. Using cookie cutters or a knife, cut festive shapes such as stars and trees. Put the cookies onto the cookie sheet, then transfer to the oven and bake for 10 minutes, or until golden brown. Remove the cookies from the oven and transfer to a wire rack, then set aside. When the cookies have cooled, drizzle over the confectioners' sugar and serve.

Hot Cross Buns

MAKES: 12

PREP: 35 MINS +
2 HRS 45 MINS
RISING

COOKING: 16-21 MINS

Ingredients

scant 4 cups strong white bread
   flour, plus extra for dusting

½ tsp salt

2 tsp ground allspice

1 tsp ground nutmeg

1 tsp ground cinnamon

2 tsp active dry yeast

¼ cup golden superfine sugar

finely grated rind of 1 lemon

scant 1¼ cups currants

scant ½ cup chopped candied peel

5½ tbsp butter, melted

1 egg

scant 1 cup tepid milk

vegetable oil, for brushing

CROSSES

6 tbsp all-purpose flour

2 tbsp butter, cut into pieces

1 tbsp cold water

GLAZE

3 tbsp milk

3 tbsp golden superfine sugar

Sift the flour, salt, and spices into a bowl and stir in the yeast, sugar, lemon rind, currants, and candied peel. Make a well in the center. In a separate bowl, mix the melted butter, egg, and milk. Pour into the dry ingredients and mix to make a soft dough, adding more milk if necessary. Brush a bowl with oil. Turn the dough out onto a floured counter and knead for 10 minutes, or until smooth and elastic. Place the dough in the oiled bowl, cover with plastic wrap, and let stand in a warm place for 1¾-2 hours, or until doubled in size.

Turn out onto a floured counter, knead for 1-2 minutes, then divide into 12 balls. Place on a greased cookie sheet, flatten slightly, then cover with oiled plastic wrap. Let stand in a warm place for 45 minutes, or until doubled in size. Preheat the oven to 425°F/220°C.

To make the crosses, sift the flour into a bowl and rub in the butter. Stir in the cold water to make a dough. Divide into 24 strips, 7-inches/18-cm long. To make the glaze, place the milk and sugar in a pan over low heat and stir until the sugar has dissolved. Brush some of the glaze over the buns and lay the dough strips on them to form crosses. Bake in the oven for 15-20 minutes, or until golden. Brush with the remaining glaze and return to the oven for 1 minute. Cool on a wire rack.

Cinnamon & Currant Loaf

SERVES: 8

PREP: 25 MINS +
1 HR
COOLING

COOKING: 1 HR 10 MINS

Ingredients

5½ oz/150 g butter, cut into
   small pieces, plus extra
   for greasing

2¼ cups all-purpose flour

pinch of salt

1 tbsp baking powder

1 tbsp ground cinnamon

generous ⅝ cup brown sugar

1 cup currants

finely grated rind of 1 orange

5-6 tbsp orange juice

6 tbsp milk

2 eggs, lightly beaten

Preheat the oven to 350°F/180°C. Grease a 2 lb/900 g loaf pan and line the bottom with parchment paper.

Sift the flour, salt, baking powder, and cinnamon into a bowl. Rub in the butter with your fingers until the mixture resembles coarse bread crumbs.

Stir in the sugar, currants, and orange rind. Beat the orange juice, milk and eggs together and add to the dry ingredients. Mix well. Spoon into the pan and make a slight dip in the center to help it rise evenly.

Bake in the preheated oven for 1-1 hour 10 minutes, or until a fine metal skewer inserted into the center of the loaf comes out clean. Let the loaf cool in the pan for 10 minutes, then turn out onto a wire rack to cool completely before slicing and serving.

Crown Loaf

MAKES: 1 LOAF

PREP: 1 HR 30 MINS

COOKING: 30 MINS

Ingredients

2 tbsp butter, cut into small pieces, plus extra for greasing

generous 1½ cups white bread flour

½ tsp salt

1 sachet active dry yeast

½ cup lukewarm milk

1 egg, lightly beaten

FILLING

4 tbsp butter, softened

¼ cup brown sugar

2 tbsp chopped hazelnuts

1 tbsp chopped preserved ginger

⅓ cup mixed candied peel

1 tbsp rum or brandy

1 cup icing confectioners' sugar

2 tbsp lemon juice

Grease a cookie sheet. Strain the flour and salt into a bowl. Stir in the yeast. Rub in the butter with your fingertips. Add the milk and egg and mix to form a dough.

Place the dough in a greased bowl, cover, and stand in a warm place for 40 minutes until doubled in size. Punch down the dough lightly for 1 minute. Roll out to a rectangle about 12 x 9 inches/ 30 x 23 cm.

To make the filling, cream together the butter and sugar until light and fluffy. Stir in the hazelnuts, ginger, candied peel, and rum or brandy. Spread the filling over the dough, leaving a 1-inch/2.5-cm border.

Roll up the dough, starting from one of the long edges, into a sausage shape. Cut into slices at 2-inch/5-cm intervals and place in a circle on the cookie sheet with the slices just touching. Cover and stand in a warm place to rise for 30 minutes.

Bake in a preheated oven, 325°F/190°C, for 20-30 minutes or until golden. Meanwhile, mix the confectioners' sugar with enough lemon juice to form a thin frosting.

Let the loaf cool slightly before drizzling with frosting. Let the frosting set slightly before serving.

Stollen

SERVES: 10

PREP: 30 MINS +
5 HRS
RISING

COOKING: 40 MINS

Ingredients

generous ½ cup currants

⅓ cup raisins

2 tbsp chopped candied peel

¼ cup candied cherries, rinsed, dried, and quartered

2 tbsp rum

2 oz/55 g butter

¾ cup milk

2 tbsp golden superfine sugar

generous 2¾ cups strong white bread flour, plus extra for dusting

½ tsp ground nutmeg

½ tsp ground cinnamon

seeds from 3 cardamoms

2 tsp active dry yeast

finely grated rind of 1 lemon

1 egg, beaten

scant ½ cup slivered almonds

vegetable oil, for brushing

6 oz/175 g marzipan

melted butter, for brushing

sifted confectioners' sugar, for dredging

Place the currants, raisins, peel, and cherries in a bowl, stir in the rum and set aside. Place the butter, milk, and sugar in a pan over low heat and stir until the sugar dissolves and the butter melts. Cool until lukewarm. Sift the flour, nutmeg, and cinnamon into a bowl. Crush the cardamom seeds and add them. Stir in the yeast. Make a well in the center, stir in the milk mixture, lemon rind, and egg and beat into a dough.

Turn the dough out onto a floured counter. Knead for 5 minutes, adding more flour if necessary. Knead in the soaked fruit and the almonds. Transfer to a clean, oiled bowl. Cover with plastic wrap and let stand in a warm place for up to 3 hours, or until doubled in size. Turn out onto a floured counter, knead for 1-2 minutes, then roll out to a 10-inch/25-cm square.

Roll the marzipan into a sausage shorter than the length of the dough. Place in the center. Fold the dough over the marzipan, overlapping it. Seal the ends. Place seam-side down on a greased cookie sheet, cover with oiled plastic wrap, and let stand in a warm place for up to 2 hours, or until doubled in size. Preheat the oven to 375°F/190°C. Bake for 40 minutes, or until golden and hollow-sounding when tapped. Brush with melted butter, dredge with confectioners' sugar and cool on a wire rack.

Special Day Bakes

Entertaining friends and family is great when everything goes with a swing, but can be quite hectic and stressful to plan and prepare. Before you start, it's worth reminding yourself that your guests will really appreciate your freshly-baked treats from the moment they arrive and smell the tantalising aroma coming from your kitchen. They'll be concentrating on the delights of good home baking and certainly won't be marking your achievements on a score card.

There are two main guidelines for success – don't be too ambitious and plan well in advance, down to the smallest detail. Always choose something you are confident about making and be realistic about your time. A frazzled wreck who has been up half the night making pastry or whisking egg whites is never going to be the hostess with the mostest!

This section gives some ideas for four occasions and can be easily adapted for most social gatherings.

Morning Coffee with Friends

Fresh Croissants
p 96-97

Coffee Streusel Cake
p 16-17

Cappuccino Squares
p 55

Classic Oatmeal Cookies
p 38-39

Afternoon Tea with the Family

Cherry Scones
p 76

Rich Fruit Cake
p 22-23

Victoria Sandwich Cake
p 12-13

Chelsea Buns
p 77

Kids' Party Time

Gingerbread People
p 46-47

Party Cookies
p 158-159

Triple Chocolate
Muffins
p 36

Lemon Butterfly
Cakes
p 48-49

An Occasion to Impress

Cheese Straws
p 114-115

Banoffee Pie
p 65

Manhattan
Cheesecake
p 66-67

Strawberry
Chocolate Gâteau
p 144-145

INDEX

apples
  apple and blackberry crumble 29
  apple and cinnamon muffins 37
  apple shortcakes 80-81
  apricot slices 82-83
  cheese and apple tart 120-121
  spiced apple tart 134-135
  traditional apple pie 28
apricots
  apricot slices 82-83
  chocolate panforte 71

bacon and cornmeal muffins 106-107
Bakewell tart 33
bananas
  banoffee pie 65
  carrot cake 14-15
blackberries
  apple and blackberry crumble 29
  forest fruit pie 64
blueberries
  blueberry clafoutis 62-63
  blueberry and lemon drizzle cake 24-25
  forest fruit pie 64
  Manhattan cheesecake 66-67

carrot cake 14-15
cheese
  carrot cake 14-15
  cheese and apple tart 120-121
  cheese and chive biscuits 104
  cheese muffins 108-109
  cheese and mustard biscuits 105
  cheese and peanut crescents 118-119
  cheese and rosemary sables 113
  cheese straws 114-115
  cheesy bread 102-103
  chocolate and cherry tiramisù 140-141
  dried cherry cheesecake muffins 34-35
  Manhattan cheesecake 66-67
  pesto palmiers 117
  savory curried crackers 112
  spiced cocktail bites 116
  strawberry roulade 68-69

Chelsea buns 77

cherries
  cherry biscuits 76
  cherry and walnut cookies 42-43
  chocolate and cherry tiramisù 140-141
  dried cherry cheesecake muffins 34-35
chives
  cheese and chive biscuits 104
  cheesy bread 102-103
chocolate
  baked chocolate Alaska 146-147
  banoffee pie 65
  cappuccino squares 55
  caramel chocolate shortbread 85
  chocolate and cherry tiramisù 140-141
  chocolate chip flapjacks 51
  chocolate drop cookies 45
  chocolate fudge cake 74-75
  chocolate panforte 71
  chocolate Viennese fingers 88-89
  cup cakes 132
  dark and white chocolate torte 136-137
  double chocolate brownies 52-53
  double chocolate chip cookies 152-153
  lebkuchen 162
  Mississippi mud cake 18-19
  nutty chocolate drizzles 92-93
  profiteroles 142-143
  raspberry dessert cake 70
  raspberry vacherin 138
  sachertorte 126-127
  strawberry chocolate gâteau 144-145
  triple chocolate muffins 36
  Yule log 130-131
Christmas cake 124-125
Christmas shortbread 160-161
cinnamon
  apple and cinnamon muffins 37
  apple shortcakes 80-81
  apricot slices 82-83
  cinnamon and currant loaf 166-167
  cinnamon rolls 78-79
  doughnut muffins 110-111
  lebkuchen 162
  panforte di Siena 128-129
  preserved ginger cake 20-21
  stollen 170-171

coffee
  cappuccino squares 55
  chocolate and cherry tiramisù 140-141
  coffee streusel cake 16-17
  sachertorte 126-127
corn syrup and molasses
  caramel chocolate shortbread 85
  chewy golden cookies 90-91
  chocolate chip flapjacks 51
  chocolate fudge cake 74-75
  Christmas cake 124-125
  cup cakes 132
  double chocolate brownies 52-53
  gingerbread people 46-47
  gingersnaps 44
  party cookies 158-159
  preserved ginger cake 20-21
  rich fruit cake 22-23
  Yuletide cookies 163
cornmeal
  bacon and cornmeal muffins 106-107
  cheese muffins 108-109
crème brûlée tarts 72-73
croissants 96-97
curry powder
  cheese straws 114-115
  savory curried crackers 112
  spiced cocktail bites 116

dates and prunes
  cheese and apple tart 120-121
  Christmas cake 124-125
  rich fruit cake 22-23
  sticky toffee sponge 30
dried and glacé fruit
  apricot slices 82-83
  Chelsea buns 77
  cherry biscuits 76
  cherry and walnut cookies 42-43
  chocolate chip flapjacks 51
  chocolate panforte 71
  Christmas cake 124-125
  cinnamon and currant loaf 166-167
  crown loaf 168-169
  Easter cookies 156-157
  fruity flapjacks 50

giggle cake 133
hot cross buns 164-165
lebkuchen 162
nutty chocolate drizzles 92-93
panforte di Siena 128-129
rich fruit cake 22-23
sticky toffee sponge 30
stollen 170-171
teacakes 98-99
traditional spiced cookies 154
see also mincemeat

Easter cookies 156-157
equipment 6-8

flapjacks 50-51
fruit preserves and jellies
    Bakewell tart 33
    roly poly pudding 31
    sachertorte 126-127

ginger
    crown loaf 168-169
    gingerbread people 46-47
    gingersnaps 44
    panforte di Siena 128-129
    preserved ginger cake 20-21
    Yuletide cookies 163
grapes: mincemeat and grape jalousie 148-149

honey
    chocolate panforte 71
    panforte di Siena 128-129
    spiced apple tart 134-135
hot cross buns 164-165

ice cream: baked chocolate Alaska 146-147

lebkuchen 162
lemons
    blueberry and lemon drizzle cake 24-25
    lemon butterfly cakes 48-49
    lemon drops 86
    lemon jumbles 87
    lemon meringue pie 32
    spiced apple tart 134-135
    tarte au citron 58-59

meringue
    baked chocolate Alaska 146-147
    lemon meringue pie 32
    mixed fruit pavlova 139
    raspberry vacherin 138
mincemeat
    festive mince pies 150-151
    mincemeat crumble bars 155
    mincemeat and grape jalousie 148-149
Mississippi mud cake 18-19
mustard
    cheese and mustard biscuits 105
    cheesy bread 102-103

nuts
    almond and hazelnut gâteau 26-27
    apricot slices 82-83
    Bakewell tart 33
    banoffee pie 65
    blueberry and lemon drizzle cake 24-25
    carrot cake 14-15
    cheese and apple tart 120-121
    cheese and peanut crescents 118-119
    cherry and walnut cookies 42-43
    chocolate fudge cake 74-75
    chocolate panforte 71
    Christmas cake 124-125
    coffee streusel cake 16-17
    crown loaf 168-169
    double chocolate chip cookies 152-153
    forest fruit pie 64
    hazelnut squares 54
    lebkuchen 162
    mincemeat crumble bars 155
    nutty chocolate drizzles 92-93
    panforte di Siena 128-129
    peanut butter cookies 40-41
    stollen 170-171

oats
    chewy golden cookies 90-91
    chocolate chip flapjacks 51
    classic oatmeal cookies 38-39
    fruity flapjacks 50
    nutty chocolate drizzles 92-93
    peanut butter cookies 40-41
    traditional spiced cookies 154

panforte di Siena 128-129

peaches
    mixed fruit pavlova 139
    peach and strawberry tart 60-61
pesto palmiers 117
profiteroles 142-143

raspberries
    forest fruit pie 64
    raspberry dessert cake 70
    raspberry vacherin 138
    roly poly pudding 31
recipe tips 9
rosemary: cheese and rosemary sables 113

sachertorte 126-127
seeds, edible
    cheese straws 114-115
    spiced cocktail bites 116
shortbread 84-85, 160-161
spices
    Chelsea buns 77
    chocolate panforte 71
    Christmas cake 124-125
    coffee streusel cake 16-17
    hot cross buns 164-165
    lebkuchen 162
    rich fruit cake 22-23
    spiced apple tart 134-135
    traditional spiced cookies 154
    Yuletide cookies 163
sticky toffee sponge 30
stollen 170-171
strawberries
    mixed fruit pavlova 139
    peach and strawberry tart 60-61
    strawberry chocolate gâteau 144-145
    strawberry roulade 68-69
    Victoria sponge 12-13

teacakes 98-99
tomatoes: sun-dried tomato rolls 100-101

Victoria sponge 12-13

Yule log 130-131
Yuletide cookies 163